Masculinities and the Adult Male Prison Experience

Jennifer Anne Sloan

Masculinities and the Adult Male Prison Experience

palgrave
macmillan

Jennifer Anne Sloan
Department of Law and Criminology
Sheffield Hallam University
Sheffield, UK

Masculinities and the Adult Male Prison Experience
ISBN 978-1-137-39914-4   ISBN 978-1-137-39915-1   (eBook)
DOI 10.1057/978-1-137-39915-1

Library of Congress Control Number: 2016939255

Cover illustration: © Photocase Addicts GmbH / Alamy Stock Photo

Printed on acid-free paper

This Palgrave Macmillan imprint is published by Springer Nature
The registered company is Macmillan Publishers Ltd. London

To Mum, Dad, James, and Chris.
In loving memory of Alan Pote.

Preface

Earlier today, I was looking through the various posts that my friends and family had put on Facebook, and one particular post caught my eye: one of my aunts observed that many of the people being shown on international news reports about the Syrian refugee crisis were disproportionately healthy, fit young men. I found this particularly thought-provoking—not least because I (someone who writes about the dominance of young men in the criminal justice system) had not actually noticed. I had done what so many of us do when watching the news or reading the press: I had picked up on the exceptions—the children and the women. People did similar things when watching the pictures of the London riots in 2011: we noticed the girls and failed to focus on the overwhelming number of young men being shown on our screens. When discussing the rise of ISIS/ISL, few ask why so many young men have gone to fight for such a cause, yet young jihadi brides cause a moral panic.

This masculine blind spot is a problem for a number of reasons. It fails to acknowledge or problematise the importance of masculinity in the criminal justice system—men's roles as both offenders *AND* victims is underplayed and underanalysed. Such preference for viewing only the women or the exceptional also skews our views of the problem—feminists have acknowledged this imposition of double deviance upon women who commit crimes for years (Heidensohn et al. 1985). But the main problem is that, if we do not SEE the men, how can we (a) help them, and (b) address the masculine identities that lead to such domi-nance of the criminal justice system? Men are clearly there, and clearly the majority of the fodder of the criminal justice system. (Indeed, if we removed men from the criminal justice system, there would be very few offenders—or officials—left!)

This book puts the spotlight on men in one of the most masculine institutions of the system—prisons—and aims to start the process of challenging masculinity, and of seeing its role in the prison experience. It is a start.

Sheffield, UK   Jennifer Anne Sloan
September 2015   j.sloan@shu.ac.uk

Acknowledgements

None of this would have been possible without the kindness and patience of the men and women within the prison that I researched—both the staff and prisoners gave me an education that I will never forget and will always appreciate. Many thanks too to Charlotte Weinberg at *Safe Ground*.

Many thanks to the University of Sheffield, who funded the doctoral research upon which this is based (Sloan 2011). Particular thanks must go to Maggie Wykes and Stephen Farrell (my doctoral supervisors); and to Joanna Shapland, Gwen Robinson, Matthew Hall, Matthew Bacon, Anna Hescott, Sara Grace, Charlotte Baxter, Gilly Sharpe, Kate Wilkinson, Tony Ellis, Cormac Behan, and Rebecca Sanders for pushing me along to get here. Thanks also to Joe Sim for telling me to get on with it all those years ago at a conference, Ben Raikes for his insights, and Lizbeth Marsh for pulling me through!

Thanks also to all my new colleagues at Sheffield Hallam, who have been supportive and patient to the nth degree whilst I got this done. It has been a pleasure working with you all. Particular thanks to Sital Dhillon, Sunita Toor, Vicky Heap, James Banks, Jake Phillips, David Best, Sarah Goodwin, Paula Hamilton, Catrin Andersson, Kathy Albertson, Jamie Irving, Liz Austen, Simon Feasey, Tanya Miles-Berry, Jamie Grace, and Shawna McCoy.

Dominic, Jules, and Harriet—thank you for all your hard work with me on this project. Working with academics is much like herding cats, but you are the best (and extremely patient) shepherds!

Mum and Dad—as ever, thank you for all you do.

James, you are my rock—thank you.

Contents

1

An Introduction to the Book

Men dominate crime, criminal justice, and imprisonment. More men commit crime, and more men work in the criminal justice system, than women. Whichever side of the law men find themselves upon, they can be sure to accrue some masculine credentials by virtue of being part of a system that is suffused with institutional masculinity (see Ellis et al. 2013). Yet, the very nature of being a man and the masculine identities of prisoners are often taken for granted in analyses of prison and imprisonment, rather than being key variables in the experience (Wykes and Welsh 2009).

This book directly engages with this knowledge gap, addressing a number of issues regarding the adult male prison experience in terms of how the process of imprisonment shapes the individual's masculine identity, and vice versa. It gives particular consideration to the masculinities of male prisoners, both as individuals, and as situated within a prisoner collective. In this book, the main interest is with the general and everyday experiences of male inmates and the relationships they have with themselves and others in terms of their masculine subjective identities. It is about the ways in which men can be and act as men in an environment devoid of many of the accoutrements of masculine living, which

© The Editor(s) (if applicable) and The Author(s) 2016   **1**
J.A. Sloan, *Masculinities and the Adult Male Prison Experience*,
DOI 10.1057/978-1-137-39915-1_1

in many ways acts to shift men from the dominant gendered position of 'man' to the dominated, submissive, and controlled feminine. It is curious that male prisons appear to be such hypermasculine spaces, when in reality they often impose highly feminising processes and positions upon the men inside. This goes some way to explaining why men in prison often undertake such highly masculinised behaviours—as Ricciardelli et al. note with regard to the Canadian prison context, 'prisoners try to respond to uncertainty and perceived risk in ways that present their masculinity as empowered rather than submissive' (2015: 492).

Gender—masculinity in particular—is the central notion of this book. As such, whereas much research on male prisoners focuses upon identity roles and relationships other than gender, this work is original in that it is simply about men and how they adapt to prison, and how prison impacts upon them as men, both negatively and, a notion that is rarely engaged with, positively. It is about how they, as men, see themselves and others— so about relationships and collectivities—but also about what they value and what they find painful—so also about their individual selves. It is about how men constitute and perform their masculine identities when isolated from many of the usual mechanisms and props that, so often in criminological research, divert attention away from the men at the centre of offending and imprisonment. It highlights the importance of control, performance, and visibility, and brings to the fore the role of the audience in men's decisions as to how to be men. In addition, another often hidden element within the criminological research process—the researcher—is brought back into the picture through the use of researcher gender as an extra dimension through which to examine participants' identities and responses to others and their situations.

The Research

The research investigates the male prison experience, and the issues of masculinity that are raised through incarceration, addressing the concern that, if crime is a potential resource for 'doing gender' (Messerschmidt 1993: 84), especially when other legitimate resources are unavailable, then how do men accomplish their masculinities? In particular, how do men achieve masculinities in an environment such as the prison, where they are deprived from more legitimate gender resources (Sykes 1958), particularly in light of the additional pressures put upon men in terms of their expected masculine performances (West and Zimmerman 1987; Butler 1990) in the eyes of other men (Kimmel 1994)? Consideration is given to how men in prison are made to perform their masculine identities in ways that are very different to how they would be expected to behave outside, mainly due to the fact that such resources for establishing masculine self (family, work, heterosexual relations, etc.) are unavailable or restricted within the prison setting, and the key audience(s) for masculine performance are highly masculine gazers. Thought is also given to how prison places men in the feminine position in so many unseen ways—unexpected in such a hypermasculine environment.

This research directly investigates the effects of the prison as an institution upon adult men, looking at their masculine identities, interactions, and experiences. This was achieved by undertaking 31 semi-structured interviews with incarcerated men, and through observations and reflections (in the form of research diaries) of the prison setting, which occurred during the four-month fieldwork period in an adult male category C training prison. The resultant qualitative data was analysed using theories of masculinities as an explanatory framework to explore the under-researched concept that criminality is dominated by *men*, and therefore most prisoners are *men*, yet little is asked or understood about the *men* who commit crimes and end up incarcerated, or the masculinities they hold. The project is distinctive on a number of levels, but primarily because the majority of studies of the prison fail to address the masculinities that lie at the heart of the institution, looking at other variables such as class, race, age, and so on, instead of the key distinctive feature—the dominance of men (who make up 95 % of prisoners in England and Wales). The book aims to satisfy the need for greater attention to the gendered dimensions of the penal system and ordinary men's experiences of it (rather than simply focusing upon extreme examples that sensationalise crime and criminology), in addition to addressing the need for wider attention to be given to the prison experience as a whole, rather than merely focusing upon the negative aspects. In addition, the research draws upon reflexive processes by including the researcher's perspectives on the gendered prison experience in order to add to the understanding of the gendered nature of the prison. The research diaries kept allowed an extra dimension of gender to be gleaned—not least because the young female researcher's gender was often used as a juxtaposing force for prisoners to 'bounce' their masculinities off—in addition to placing the researcher firmly within the subjective research context.

Moreover, the informing interest here is the mature (but not aged) masculinity so poorly understood within crime, criminality, and beyond. Such are the differences between male and female offenders that men's position within the prison system is seen as 'normal' and in keeping with masculine traits of aggression, dominance, and deviance. Men are viewed in this way to such an extent that their gender becomes invisible—the term *prisoner* becomes assumed to mean *male prisoner* (Wykes and Welsh 2009: 57); thus, analysing adult men's experiences of incarceration explicitly as male/masculine (as opposed to detailed and distinguished features of male offending such as youth, drugs, violence, ethnicity and race, etc.) addresses the annihilation and undermining of gender in much work and debate surrounding men's prisons and criminality. The men in the prison, albeit diverse in terms of background, ethnicity, race, age, and so on, had one overarching commonality. They were, first and foremost, *men*.

Masculinities

There are many different approaches to the study of masculinity/masculinities, which can be hugely problematic when actually trying to reach a common understanding of theoretical approach. This book comes from the following theoretical standpoint:

1. Following Connell's work (2005), this book conforms to the idea of **hegemonic masculinities**—that being the idea that masculinity fluctuates in different times and spaces, yet there is always a hegemonic position to which other men aspire. Men compete against each other for masculine achievement.
2. At the same time, it is recognised that there is not one single masculinity—instead we follow Connell again to think in terms of **pluralities of masculinities**.

3. These masculinities are embodied and performed: gender is seen as a **social construction**, which is created in relation to the genders of others (Connell 2005); masculinity is a process which is 'done' (West and Zimmerman 1987; Butler 1990).

4. Such performances and embodiments are achieved through the **resources** available to that individual against which to relate his masculine self. Such resources include personal corporeality, other people and their genders and bodies, consumable goods, money, positions of power, and so on.

5. **Crime is a resource** through which to perform masculinity, generally when other, more socially legitimate and approved resources are unavailable to that individual (Messerschmidt 1993: 84).

6. These performances are directed towards an **audience**. Kimmel (1994) suggests that masculine identity is enacted for the benefit of other men and in order to receive some form of approval from the male collective. This definition is of particular value when considering the prison environment, where men are situated close to other men (both prisoners and staff) and alter their behaviours for the benefit of what others can see, and who those others are. In this book, I argue that there are others that the individual sees to be important as audiences in the masculine performance, not just other men.

7. The **audience that matters** to an individual at a particular point in their life is subject to change; as such, the performances of masculinity may also change in response to the different people who matter that are watching him.

8. Such performances are subject to particular **challenges** in the prison through a lack of performative resources available to the men, along with the feminising processes that the prison imposes.

In addition, the multitude of different definitions of masculinity can often result in some confusion about what we actually mean by the term itself. With that in mind, I thought it wise to define exactly what is meant in this book when referring to notions of masculinity. Within this text, masculinity is posited in line with Connell's (2005) notion: that is, a social construct. The term refers to those aspects of men's lives that they take on to demonstrate their own maleness to others and to themselves—and it changes from man to man depending upon the expectations of the audience he is acting out his gendered self for. It is highly subjective on the one hand, but guided by underlying cultural and social expectations that run through our society on the other. As such, it is both individually and collectively formulated.

Prison is perhaps one of the best examples of a closed 'gendered institution'—where 'gender is present in the processes, practices, images and ideologies, and distributions of power in the various sectors of social life' (Acker 1992: 567). All inmates are of a single sex, as are the majority of staff members, although this is changing following the advent of 'cross-posting' in 1982 (see Tait 2008: 64). Much existing work takes gender for granted rather than an aspect of identity that is constantly in flux and constructed over the lifespan (Hollway 1989).[1] The process by which an inmate will interpret and perform his own masculine identity will also be directly affected by his relationships: the forming of one's identity is a consequence of experiences had with others and the context of the observing 'audience' and how they are interpreted, whether these 'others' are family, friends, foes, or complete strangers.

Where research on masculinity in prison has been done (see the work of Yvonne Jewkes, Ben Crewe, and Coretta Phillips, to name but three), it is often masculinity-in-combination: rather than placing masculinity in the spotlight, other themes of importance are highlighted and foregrounded, such as race, power, or experience. Whilst these are significant and salient issues, this approach runs the risk of sidelining the ultimate connector of everyone in male prisons in favour of variables that differentiate.

Relationships between staff and inmates have been widely investigated and documented (Liebling and Price 1999; Liebling and Arnold 2004; Crawley 2004; Crewe 2006a), as has the concept of the prison culture and correctional communities in early works from the USA (Clemmer 1958; Sykes 1958; Irwin and Cressey 1962; Simon 2000). What has not

---

[1] Sadly, the majority of work that does directly engage with masculinity in the criminal justice system is left at the MA/PhD stage (Aresti 2010; Bell 2012; Butler 2007; Hefner 2009; Moolman 2011; de Viggiani 2003; Whitehead 2000 for instance). There is a clear question to be asked about why such promising studies rarely continue beyond the doctoral stage—it is clear that there is not enough value being placed upon this topic to encourage early year researchers to continue along the research path.

been greatly considered is the relationship between the male inmate and his identity and how this affects how male individuals interact with others *and* how they experience and interpret imprisonment. The issue has been looked at somewhat in reverse: coping strategies for the painful experiences of imprisonment that include various social strategies have been given some thought (Sykes 1956; Clemmer 1958; Sykes and Messinger 1960; Stanko 2001; Reuss 2003; Wilson 2004; Crewe 2005a), along with theories of conformity to inmate codes and existing social structures (Wheeler 1961; Irwin and Cressey 1962; Jacobs 1974); however, this fails to recognise how distinct relationships play a role in both defining and coping with the experience of imprisonment on both an interpersonal and an internal gendered level (there tends to be a focus upon the interrelation of individual relationships to form an overall social system [Garabedian 1963]). In addition, the majority of this research is dated and so somewhat obsolete in the modern English and Welsh penal estate when considering the temporal and geographical fluctuations in societal composition and values. By considering such issues in the modern penal context, a better understanding of men and their interactions and performances has been achieved, which enables a better understanding of male behaviours on individual and collective bases.

In addition to looking into masculinities and crime, this study looks at masculine identity on a wider scale from a female perspective, through the eyes of a female researcher. This is a concept rarely considered in wider criminological study, where the historical tradition has been for male academics to study male penal institutions (Propper 1989: 57), the concept of masculinity being lost to the realm of 'obviousness'. Many describe the prison setting as being a male space (Bandyopadhyay 2006; Evans and Wallace 2008), fitting into the sphere that is 'historically developed by men, currently dominated by men, and symbolically interpreted from the standpoint of men in leading positions, both in the present and historically' (Acker 1992: 567). Yet, masculinity is a particularly consequential concept in the process of discussing incarcerated men: for many, it is 'illegitimate' expressions of this masculinity that have resulted in their incarceration in the first place.

Why Is Masculinity Important in the Criminal Justice System?

When first undertaking this research, friends and colleagues often asked me questions like 'why men?' or 'why aren't you looking at women's prisons?', as if (a) masculinities was not my realm, or (b) I would be more comfortable researching women as a woman. For too long men have researched men and missed the subtleties of masculine identity, and feminist criminologists need to place men more into the foreground of prisons research due to their huge numbers, dominance of normative discourses regarding incarceration, and the fact that men are often at the heart of female prisoners' pains. Men dominate crime and imprisonment, but are rarely clearly *seen* due to their being normalised and unproblematised as a gender.

For example, if one gives consideration to the purposes of sentencing, as defined in section 142 of the Criminal Justice Act 2003, a new depth of understanding can be appreciated when placing the section under a gendered lens. The section is as follows:

Purposes of Sentencing

(1) Any court dealing with an offender in respect of his offence must have regard to the following purposes of sentencing—
    (a) the punishment of offenders,
    (b) the reduction of crime (including its reduction by deterrence),
    (c) the reform and rehabilitation of offenders,
    (d) the protection of the public, and
    (e) the making of reparation by offenders to persons affected by their offences. (Criminal Justice Act 2003 s142)

When one applies the idea that we are not so much punishing offenders, as punishing their incorrect implementation and performance of masculinity (i.e. through crime rather than legitimate means), none of the purposes of sentencing actually go any way towards addressing such masculinities. *Retribution* merely states that these are 'bad men'. *Crime reduction and deterrence* become highly problematic when one views prison as a potential bastion of masculinity (although we shall see later that this hypermasculine image is often in response to processes of feminisation). *Reform and rehabilitation* imply there will be a positive masculinity to 'return' to or impose—highly problematic when considering the entrenched nature of patriarchy and misogyny within society. *Public protection* can hardly be achieved through sustaining an institution that prioritises negative masculine performances; and *reparation* will do little to address negative masculinities apart from potentially humiliating (see Pamment and Ellis 2010 regarding wearing high-visibility clothing when undertaking reparative community work) or impacting upon potential consumer masculinity by taking away potential buying power (see Crewe 2009: 277), leading men to have their masculine performativities placed under even greater threat.

With reference to rehabilitation on a gendered level, very little attention is granted to matters of gender with respect to operational prison policy, although there is one publication specifically concerning a prison group work programme focusing upon masculinity, reported by the West Yorkshire Probation Service some years ago (Potts 1996).[2] The aims of these sessions were to enhance male awareness and challenging of belief systems that enable the abuse of women and children; to make men aware of the learned nature of gender roles; to aid in the understanding of the interactions between behaviours and negative beliefs; and to encourage debate on the matter (1996: 10). The sessions were to provide a safe space for male prisoners to open up and discuss emotions that may not be acceptable outside this arena, and to allow men to see the progress they are making relative to others, whilst also conforming the existence—and perhaps previously unacknowledged flexibility—of gendered behavioural and value stereotypes and the learned nature of manhood (1996: 27).

The programme itself sounds highly positive and innovative—despite acknowledgement that it has a restrictive view in terms of avoiding engagement with matters of race and sexuality, and requiring support systems for staff (and the associated gender difficulties in the management

---

[2] I found this in a cupboard within the OMU of the prison I was researching.

of such a programme) (1996: 30). Unfortunately, it is not currently an accredited offending behaviour programme. In fact, although the 2010–2011 annual report of the Correctional Services Accreditation Panel[3] lists a total of 49 currently accredited or recognised programmes, none of these are described as directly engaging with issues of maleness or masculinity (Ministry of Justice 2010–2011: 47–72). Many are directly focused upon male offenders, some look specifically at the promotion of prosocial behavioural models, and some target particularly gendered offending (such as sexual offending, violence, and the promotion of healthy relationships through tackling domestically violent behaviours).

Although these programmes will often be dealing with the negative manifestations of masculine identities, the major underlying factor of gender is overlooked, as was forewarned by Potts regarding the potential to address the problematisation of masculinity through the issue of domestic violence (1996: 31). Crucially though, Potts' professional work relays the fact that masculinity is an important element in the criminal justice system as recognised by professionals and academics:

> After all, if we believe that alcohol or drugs related crime can be reduced by work intended to reduce such abuse, then surely gender related crime – and that's most of it – can be reduced by developing interventions which deconstruct traditional masculinity. (1996: 31)

One organisation that does engage directly with masculinity and men in prison is *Safe Ground*. Established in 1993, this London-based organisation states that it:

> challenges people and communities to do relationships differently. Through drama, dialogue and debate, we enhance empathy and encourage expression, developing self-awareness and promoting social justice.
> *Safe Ground* is a small team with national reach and influence. We are absolutely committed to reducing the stigma faced by the families of people in prison, to improving access to and diversity of educational activities

---

[3] It is very difficult to find information regarding the work of the Correctional Services Accreditation panel, or a definitive list of those programmes that are approved.

in prisons and to creating alternatives to traditional punishment and exclusion, proven to be so ineffective. (Safe Ground 2015)

The organisation provides a number of different programmes including those targeting issues of fatherhood and the family, which they were originally commissioned to run by the Home Office.[4] Of particular interest is the programme they run called '*Man Up*', which Executive Director Charlotte Weinberg describes as a course that looks at the social norms and values impacting participants' developments as men, and the consequent lack of freedom available to them in becoming 'men'. It attempts to overcome the fact that prison is lacking in 'safe spaces' within which men can be vulnerable, and works to teach men 'how to construct a safe space in yourself that you can carry round with you and is resilient and robust enough to overcome all the slings and arrows'. The programme runs for 15 hours within 6 sessions of 8–16 men/young men in a range of settings including prisons, Youth Offender Institutions (YOIs), and community settings. It has undergone a number of evaluations finding that the programme 'impacts profoundly on participants' understanding around gender norms, enhances wellbeing, and allows men to develop less "alpha-male" attitudes (which often relate to violent responses, antisocial activities and lack of emotional engagement)' (Safe Ground 2014:1). The study also found improvements in scores pointing to well-being, positive attitudinal changes within the group, and high ratings in belief in its being an 'effective challenge to offending behaviour'.

Safe Ground also created an accompanying programme for prison officers, initially called *Professional Love*, but now renamed *Officers' Mess*, which allows prison officers space to consider how to undertake their roles as agents of the state in a manner that enables structural internal change within their charges. Throughout all their programmes, consideration has been given as to how to distinguish them from other 'interventions', in that *Safe Ground* aims to create a sustainable performance that can be carried around with the men after the intervention is over—it looks to create real attitudinal change in the men, and is not all about Key Performance Indicators (KPIs).

---

[4] It should be understood that the Home Office discussed is now a historical entity, with its role being taken over by the Ministry of Justice.

Interestingly, the *Man Up* programme considers the issues around gendered performativity that are discussed in this book, recognising the influence that other individuals have over a man's choices and actions—Charlotte Weinberg made a thought-provoking point in stating: "Sometimes choices aren't choices, they're dilemmas' (Weinberg 2005, personal communication). What *Man Up* seems to aim to do is to bring the element of control back into men's lives—the safe space that the programme facilitates within the men undertaking the programme allows the men to have somewhere within which to make choices for themselves, emulating and mimicking the thinking space that prison can sometimes provide. It tries to form an identity within the men that is safe and secure in which the men can find their own value, and therefore have an element of control over their lives. In addition, it challenges the types of men that they see themselves as, as another evaluation elucidated:

> All course completers expressed how their strong masculine identities and associated values and beliefs were challenged throughout the course, and how this prompted reflection and subsequent change. These reflections seemed to be about re-storying what a man's role should be; specifically one concerned with responsibility and accountability, rather than dominance, aggression, and assertiveness. (Blagden and Perrin 2015: 17)

Although the programmes run by *Safe Ground* are not currently accredited by the Correctional Services Accreditation Panel, they are recognised to have huge benefits to men in and out of prison. Indeed, perhaps their not being accredited is a positive as it allows a degree of flexibility and responsiveness, which is arguably necessary when addressing varying notions of masculinities. *Man Up* is delivered in seven prisons, and—at the time of writing—has been commissioned in six Youth Offending Teams (YOTs) in South and West Yorkshire and five more in Leicester. The programme has also been adapted for delivery within secure forensic units. As such, the programme taps into the key underpinning message that this book attempts to relay, the connection between men in all spheres of the incarceration journey: the fact that they are men. Yet in spite of its successes and the measured benefits of the programme to the men who have graduated from it, it is still not available throughout all male prisons in England and Wales, and is provided on a fairly ad hoc basis by an organisation with charitable status; it has not received the recognition it deserves in the realm of policy, despite sitting on numerous strategic boards in the criminal justice arena. Once again, we can see a lack of strategic prioritisation of masculinity-based programmes.[5]

It is interesting that this approach has not been taken further, particularly when we consider the importance of recognising identity and its surrounding issues in other areas of the criminal justice system—the intertwined nature of mental health issues having a key impact on identity and incarceration is common knowledge. A 2008 survey found that 62% of male sentenced prisoners had some form of personality disorder in prison (Stewart 2008). So, mental health is central to identity and prison.

Prison is central to identity. Gender is central to identity. Yet few people put these things together.

Performance

Goffman argues that 'femininity and masculinity are in a sense the prototypes of essential expression' (1976: 7). He goes on to recognise the situational character of gender, noting that 'one might just as well say there is no gender identity. There is only a schedule for the portrayal of gender' (1976: 8), and, referring to earlier work, that there are two regions of the performance of one's identity: the front region, 'the place where the performance is given' (1958: 66), and the back region or backstage: 'a place, relative to a given performance, where the impression fostered by the performance is knowingly contradicted as a matter of course' (1958: 69). So, the performance of one's identity is for the benefit of whichever audience inhabits the front stage area of an individual's life—that area which requires a degree of 'impression management' (1958: 70), a process through which an individual hides their backstage regions of self in order to control the performed self being witnessed. Although Goffman does not make particular distinctions according to gender, it is easy to

---

[5] Please note that all opinions and critiques made are done so by the author and not in any way endorsed or supported by *Safe Ground*.

see how such impression management may be tailored according to the gender of those occupying the front stage area, and the importance of a particular audience in gendered terms.

The concept of the performance and construction of the gendered identity has been considered by numerous commentators since Goffman— Tolson contended that working class masculinity was:

> a kind of 'performance'. As a boy grows up, tied to his particular audience, he develops a repertoire of stories, jokes and routines. In his external personality, he learns to reproduce the expectations of his public – their inherited ways of speaking, their attitudes and values. Overwhelmingly, what characterizes his performance is a sense of 'fatalism' – of 'taking the world as you find it' – for inside the locally-constructed working-class world there is little room for individual deviation. (1977: 43)

Butler also speaks of gender as being performative, through acts and gestures which:

> produce the effect of an internal core or substance, but produce this *on the surface* of the body, through the play of signifying absences that suggest, but never reveal, the organizing principle of identity as a cause. Such acts, gestures, enactments, generally construed, are *performative* in the sense that the essence or identity that they otherwise purport to express are *fabrications* manufactured and sustained through corporeal signs and other discursive means. (Butler 1990: 173)

Holmund (1993) even suggests (albeit with little academic detail) that masculinity is a form of masquerade, but is let down by the lack of academic interrogation of the question that if masculinity is a form of masquerade, what is the 'truth' of the issue, under the masquerade? This work retains Butler's notion of gendered identities as performed, with this performance based upon the internal gendered 'truth' regarding the individual, with the performance being the ways in which this internal state is shown to others. As such, gendered identities are constructed and scripted (on, through, and by the body) for the benefit of others, and this audience will potentially shape the chosen manufactured gender identity that is sustained by an individual. Connell seems to share this approach, stating that 'gender is not fixed in advance of social interaction, but is constructed in interaction' (2005: 35). Kimmel's contention that masculinity is both homosocial enactment and homophobia (1994) sustains this argument, contending that men act in certain ways towards other men (and women) for the purpose of proving their masculinities to other men who 'watch' and subsequently grant them their masculine status. In reality though, is it just for men? In this book, I contend that, through the lens of the female researcher, we can see things to be a little more complex.

Reflexivity

In addition to interviews, through the keeping of reflexive diaries (which also served the function of providing a source for confidential debriefing at the end of a day in the prison), the impacts of the prison setting were recorded from a gendered researcher perspective, as a young woman interviewing and observing men. Reflection upon the emotional toughness and gendered nature of working in the prison environment adds another original element to the analysis of the prison experience, in that it provides a different perspective through which to contextualise the adult male prisoner's perspectives, and a different audience for male performances. A triangulation of the experiences and perceptions of the adult male prisoner as an individual, the adult male prisoner as a member of a prisoner collective, and the adult female prison researcher, allows an in-depth analysis of the gendered aspects of the prison setting and gendered performances of identity.

The majority of researchers who have been able to gain access to, and have been interested in performing research in, the prison setting are men (Propper 1989). As such, it is easy for the issues of maleness, masculinity, and manhood to go somewhat unnoticed or taken for granted as 'normal'. By having a female researcher investigating the concept of men in prison, issues of gender can be understood from a different standpoint. Gender differences between researcher and subject offer at least some critical distance and in this instance may also ameliorate any tendency towards competitiveness evident in male-only contexts. In truth, 'free' masculinity is validated through its juxtaposition to femininity (Connell 2005: 43)—the category of 'male' requires the 'female' for validation, with gender being socially constructed in a binary fashion, an element almost entirely missing for male prisoners. Sykes makes particular note of this (and thus shows the issue to have pervaded the state of prisons throughout the ages):

> The inmate is shut off from the world of women which by its very polarity gives the male world much of its meaning. Like most men, the inmate must search for his identity not simply within himself but also in the picture of himself which he finds reflected in the eyes of others; and since a significant half of his audience is denied him, the inmate's self image is in danger of becoming half complete, fractured, a monochrome without the hues of reality. (1958: 72)

It is precisely this self-image, and the reflections perceived by the inmate, viewer, and society itself, that was of interest in this research. From a gendered perspective, the role of the female researcher was invaluable, as a degree of gender-objectivity was attainable from an observer/researcher perspective in terms of interpretations of male experience (which has been described as a 'multifaceted category' with varying effects according to interpretation—Ashe 2004: 187), and the male participants had a non-competitive space in which to discuss notions of male identity, whereby the researcher could never truly become part of the 'group', which has been seen to have negative implications for rapport and researcher identity (Horowitz 1986). The reflexive process is a central thread of the book.

The difference that gender makes in the interview process is an interesting concept, and research suggests that it can have an effect (Padfield and Procter 1996). The researcher's 'femaleness' may have enabled a degree of emotional interaction that male inmates lack when living in such an emotionally limited environment. In this way, matters of a more familiar and general nature (such as identity and interaction) could be unpicked and interpreted on different levels, with the prison being the perfect setting in which to undertake such an exploration due to its extreme gendered nature and functions. The research allows us to understand better male identities, experiences, and interactions when situated within a particularly gendered setting such as the prison. It seeks to understand the importance of others in individuals' interactions with both others and their selves.

Summary

The book combines consideration of masculinities and the modern English (adult male) penal estate, engaging with the masculinities of prisoners as a privileged theme, looking beyond other variables such as age, race, and class to what connects the individuals experiencing them—their identities as men. Further to this, looking both at the general prison experience, and considering both negatives and positives from prisoners' perspectives is different, as much research hones in on one particular element of imprisonment, or tends to focus upon the less desirable attributes and behaviours of prisoners. Finally, the triangulation of various prison experiences to include the individual, the social, *and* the female prison researcher is a new approach to prison research, engaging both with methodologies employed in traditional prison sociological studies, yet including an element of gendered reflexivity that tends to be lacking in many accounts of imprisonment.

The book begins by looking in more detail at the process of researching men in prison that guided this research, and the importance of placing the gendered researcher back into the recognised research process—too often, the researcher fails to consider their own part in the project and, when considering the fact that gender is (a) relative and (b) performative, this can lose a great amount of information regarding gendered and reactive behaviours that make up research data formed from prison ethnography. Chapters 3–5 look at the lived masculinities of men in prison that emerged from the research project as seen through the body, the impact of time, and the role of spaces on the gendered self, the relational aspects of the male prison experience, and the subsequent vulnerabilities of these men that they work so hard to hide. These chapters bring to the fore the ways in which men are placed into the feminine position in many unexpected ways.

Chapter 6 looks at the gendered prison experience as a whole, and how the different elements of masculinities seem to intersect with regard to notions of control (be that of the self or others), visibility, and a notion that I refer to as the 'audience that matters' (see also Sloan forthcoming[6]). This 'audience that matters' trope refers to the fact that, whilst men are

---

[6] Many thanks in particular to Paula Hamilton for helping me to see the significance of this issue.

constantly performing their masculinities, the audience that they perform for, and whose opinion(s) matter most to that individual, changes over the course of a man's criminal career (and, subsequently, can have implications for successful desistance from crime in the long term). Linked to notions of social capital, this idea also allows this work to connect theories of masculinity (so often lacking) to the desistance literature (although see Hamilton 2015).

The book raises a number of issues adding to the debate about the functions and understandings of imprisonment, going to the very heart of theories of punishment, by putting men back at the centre—where they have arguably always been but are rarely truly seen.

References

Acker, J. (1992). From sex roles to gendered institutions. *Contemporary Sociology, 21*(5), 565–569.

Aresti, A. (2010). *'Doing time after time': A hermeneutic phenomenological understanding of reformed ex-prisoners experiences of self-change and identity negotiation.* Unpublished PhD Thesis, Birkbeck, University of London.

Ashe, F. (2004). Deconstructing the experiential bar: Male experience and feminist resistance. *Men and Masculinities, 7*(2), 187–204.

Bandyopadhyay, M. (2006). Competing masculinities in a prison. *Men and Masculinities, 9*, 186–203.

Bell, C. (2012). *Captive masculinity: Performing masculinity in the prisons of Northern Ireland.* Unpublished MA Dissertation, Warwick University.

Blagden, N. & Perrin, C. (2015). *Evaluating the man-up programme across three London prisons: An interim report.* Retrieved November, 2015 from http://www.safeground.org.uk/wp-content/uploads/2014/04/Blagden-and-Perrin-Man-Up-Interim-Report.pdf

Butler, J. (1990). *Gender trouble: Feminism and the subversion of identity.* London and New York: Routledge.

Butler, M. (2007). *Prisoner confrontations: The role of shame, masculinity and respect.* Unpublished PhD Thesis, University of Cambridge.

Clemmer, D. (1958). *The prison community* (Newth ed.). New York: Holt, Reinhart and Winston.

Connell, R. W. (2005). *Masculinities* (2nd ed.). Cambridge: Polity Press.

Crawley, E. (2004). *Doing prison work: The public and private lives of prison officers*. Cullompton: Willan Publishing.

Crewe, B. (2005a). Prisoner society in the era of hard drugs. *Punishment and Society, 7*(4), 457–481.

Crewe, B. (2005b). Codes and conventions: The terms and conditions of contemporary inmate values. In A. Liebling & S. Maruna (Eds.), *The effects of imprisonment*. Cullompton: Willan Publishing.

Crewe, B. (2006a). Male prisoners' orientations towards female officers in an English prison. *Punishment and Society, 8*(4), 395–421.

Crewe, B. (2006b). The drugs economy and the prisoner society. In Y. Jewkes & H. Johnston (Eds.), *Prison readings: A critical introduction to prisons and imprisonment*. Cullompton: Willan Publishing.

Crewe, B. (2006c). Prison drug dealing and the ethnographic lens. *The Howard Journal, 45*(4), 347–368.

Crewe, B. (2009). *The prisoner society: Power, adaptation, and social life in an English prison*. Oxford, New York: Oxford University Press.

De Viggiani, N. (2003). *(Un)healthy prison masculinities: Theorising men's health in prison*. Unpublished PhD Thesis, University of Bristol.

Ellis, A., Sloan, J., & Wykes, M. (2013). Moatifs' of masculinity: The stories told about 'men' in British newspaper coverage of the Raoul Moat case. *Crime Media Culture, 9*(1), 3–21.

Evans, T., & Wallace, P. (2008). A prison within a prison? The masculinity narratives of male prisoners. *Men and Masculinities, 10*(4), 484–507.

Garabedian, P. G. (1963). Social roles and processes of socialization in the prison community. *Social Problems, 11*(2), 139–152.

Goffman, E. (1958). *The presentation of self in everyday life*. Edinburgh: University of Edinburgh Social Sciences Research Centre. Monograph No. 2.

Goffman, E. (1976). *Gender advertisements*. London and Basingstoke: The MacMillan Press Ltd.

Hamilton, P. (2015). *Desisting men: Narrative transitions of masculine identities*. Unpublished PhD Thesis, Sheffield Hallam University.

Hefner, M. K. (2009). *Negotiating masculinity within prison*. Unpublished MA Thesis, The University of North Carolina at Greensboro.

Holmlund, C. (1993). 'Masculinity as Multiple Masquerade', in S. Cohan and I. R. Hark, eds., *Screening the Male*. London: Routledge.

Hollway, W. (1989). *Subjectivity and method in psychology: Gender, meaning and science*. London, Newbury Park and New Delhi: Sage Publications.

Horowitz, R. (1986). Remaining an outsider: Membership as a threat to research rapport. *Urban Life, 14*(4), 409–430.

Irwin, J., & Cressey, D. R. (1962). Thieves, convicts and the inmate culture. *Social Problems, 10* (2), 142–155.

Jacobs, J. B. (1974). Street gangs behind bars. *Social Problems, 21*(3), 395–409.

Kimmel, M. S. (1994). Masculinity as homophobia: Fear, shame, and silence in the construction of gender identity. In H. Brod & M. Kaufman (Eds.), *Theorizing masculinities*. Thousand Oaks and London: Sage.

Liebling, A., & Arnold, H. (2004). *Prisons and their moral performance*. Oxford and New York: Oxford University Press.

Liebling, A., & Price, D. (1999). *An exploration of staff-prisoner relationships at HMP Whitemoor*. London: Prison Service.

Messerschmidt, J. W. (1993). *Masculinities and crime*. Maryland: Rowman and Littlefield Publishers, Inc.

Ministry of Justice. (2010–2011). *The correctional services accreditation panel report 2010–2011*. Retrieved November, 2015 from https://www.gov.uk/government/uploads/system/uploads/attachment_data/file/217276/correctional-services-acc-panel-annual-report-2010-11.pdf

Moolman, B. (2011). *Permeable boundaries: Incarcerated sex offender masculinities in South Africa*. Unpublished PhD Thesis, University of California, Davis.

Padfield, M., & Procter, I. (1996). The effect of interviewer's gender on the interviewing process: A comparative enquiry. *Sociology, 30*(2), 355–366.

Pamment, N., & Ellis, T. (2010). A retrograde step: The potential impact of high visibility uniforms within youth justice reparation. *The Howard Journal of Criminal Justice, 49*(1), 18–30.

Potts, D. (1996). *Why do men commit most crime? Focusing on masculinity in a prison group*. Wakefield, UK: West Yorkshire Probation Service.

Propper, A. M. (1989). Love, marriage, and father-son relationships among male prisoners. *The Prison Journal, 69*(2), 57–63.

Reuss, A. (2003). Taking a long hard look at imprisonment. *The Howard Journal, 42*(5), 426–436.

Ricciardelli, R., Maier, K., & Hannah-Moffat, K. (2015). Strategic masculinities: Vulnerabilities, risk and the production of prison masculinities. *Theoretical Criminology, 19*(4), 491–513.

Safe Ground. (2014). *Man up development project evaluation*. London: Safe Ground. Retrieved November, 2015 from http://www.safeground.org.uk/wp-content/uploads/2014/09/Man-Up-Development-Evaluation.pdf

Safe Ground. (2015). Retrieved November, 2015 from http://www.safeground.org.uk/about-us/who-we-are-what-we-do/

Simon, J. (2000). Th e 'Society of Captives' in the Era of hyper-incarceration. *Theoretical Criminology, 4* (3), 285–308.

Sloan, J. (Forthcoming). Aspirational masculinities. In Robinson, A. & Hamilton, P. (Eds.), *Transforming identities.*

Stanko, E. A. (2001). *Prisoners' insecurity and the culture of prisons.* Retrieved July, 2011 from http://www.iss.co.za/pubs/monographs/no29/prison.html

Stewart, D. (2008). *The problems and needs of newly sentenced prisoners: Results from a national survey.* London: Ministry of Justice.

Sykes, G. M. (1956). Men, merchants, and toughs: A study of reactions to imprisonment. *Social Problems, 4*(2), 130–138.

Sykes, G. (1958). *The society of captives: A study of a maximum security prison* (2007th ed.). Princeton, NJ: Princeton University Press.

Sykes, G. M., & Messinger, S. L. (1960). The inmate social system. In R. A. Cloward (Ed.), *Theoretical studies in social organisation of the prison.* New York: Social Science Research Council.

Tait, S. (2008). Prison officers and gender. In J. Bennett, B. Crewe, & A. Wahidin (Eds.), *Understanding prison staff.* Cullompton: Willan Publishing.

Tolson, A. (1977). *The limits of masculinity.* London: Tavistock Publications Limited.

West, C., & Zimmerman, D. H. (1987). Doing gender. *Gender and Society, 1*(2), 125–151.

Weinberg, C. (2015). Executive Director of Safe Ground, Conversation with the Author 19.10.2015, Personal Communication.

Wheeler, S. (1961). Socialization in correctional communities. *American Sociological Review, 26*(5), 697–712.

Whitehead, A. (2000). *Rethinking masculinity: a critical examination of the dynamics of masculinity in the context of an English prison.* Unpublished PhD Thesis, University of Southampton.

Wilson, D. (2004). 'Keeping Quiet' or 'Going Nuts': Strategies used by young, black, men in custody. *The Howard Journal, 43*(3), 317–330.

Wykes, M., & Welsh, K. (2009). *Violence, gender & justice.* London, Thousand Oaks, New Delhi and Singapore: Sage Publications Ltd.

2

Doing Prison Research

Introduction

The research aimed to provide insights into the manner in which imprisonment is experienced by men. By better understanding how men 'do' being in prison, where many normalising contexts and resources for performing socially legitimate masculine identities are unavailable, such as liberty, goods and services, autonomy, heterosexual relationships, and security (Sykes 1958), where men are placed into feminising positions, and where such men are literally 'captive' in such a context for the researcher, it may help to enhance the understandings of masculinities more broadly, and to help to explain its association with crime. A key focus is upon interpersonal interactions between prisoners, based upon the concept of gender and the gendered body (and its use through gestures) being 'performative' (Butler 1990: 173).

In the prison setting, the audience for such performances is made up of both staff and, more noteworthily, other prisoners, who, at least in the prisons literature, are seen to enforce quite a strict code of behaviour within the prison setting (see Newton 1994: 196; Sabo et al 2001: 10; Crewe 2005; Hsu 2005: 10). Relationships and interactions are,

© The Editor(s) (if applicable) and The Author(s) 2016   **23**
J.A. Sloan, *Masculinities and the Adult Male Prison Experience*,
DOI 10.1057/978-1-137-39915-1_2

therefore, inherently linked to gendered identities. In addition, identity is arguably concerned both with how an individual is seen by others/performs as a man (i.e. his visibility), and how he, as a man, experiences the institution and its components as an individual self.

The Fieldwork

Fieldwork was undertaken between the end of April and the start of September 2009 within an adult male category C institution. Thirty-one in-depth, semi-structured interviews were performed from a self-selecting sample of participants, each lasting on average approximately an hour (being scheduled in line with the routine of the prison), with various themes and questions that should be covered in the course of the interview, in addition to more flexible periods of conversation or narrative that emerged. The methodology of interviewing prisoners was chosen as this was felt to be the best (and only) real manner in which to investigate the experiences of men in prison in any detail through which gendered dimensions could be seen. Individual interviews by a female researcher with male inmates, whilst both 'an opportunity for signifying masculinity and a peculiar type of encounter in which masculinity is threatened' (Schwalbe and Wolkomir 2001: 91), were preferred to focus groups, where the need for individuals to undertake gendered performances for the other men in the group within the prison context, where the maintenance of a tough exterior in lieu of emotions and feelings is given priority, might have been greater.

By being present within the institution and showing a clear interest in prisoners as people, a better relationship was established with many participants, which resulted in a deeper understanding of the situation. In addition, by being in the institution, the extra layer of data regarding the researcher experience was obtained (though unexpectedly), which, albeit not contingent upon an interview methodology, certainly was linked closely with it in terms of the emotional responses to prisoners' stories. As such, I tried to address Phillips and Earle's argument for 'greater inclusion of the positional subjectivities of the researchers, as well as those of the subaltern and marginalized prisoners' (2010: 375).

The interviews were performed with determinate and indeterminate (life and IPP[1]) sentenced prisoners, spanning a 35-year age range with an average age of 31. The process of recruitment and sampling chosen began with the use of posters being displayed on the wings and in various other communal spaces around the prison, advertising the project to prisoners and inviting their expressions of interest using reply slips sent to the psychology department. This opportunistic sampling method did produce a good initial sample of prisoners, but had numerous drawbacks in terms of shaping the sample in favour of those who actually looked at the posters and who could read and understand them. In addition, the sample was made up of prisoners who wished to speak with me. Although ethically and emotionally this was the most appropriate group of people to interview, the individuals who did express an interest may well have had very different characteristics to those who did not, or may have had a particular axe to grind or experiences to share, and thus this may have placed a limitation upon the generalisability of the results.

Periods of time were spent on the prison wings, interacting with staff and prisoners and observing what went on and the general routine of the jail, with this data feeding into a reflexive diary. Various administrative tasks, including putting psychology files into order, collecting post, organising psychology book collections, helping to produce OMU[2] identity/appointment cards for prisoner use, etc, were undertaken, all of which set up some rapport with staff, leading to enhanced access to areas such as the wings and the segregation unit. All of this helped with the contextualisation of prisoner narratives. Some prisoners volunteered for the study after they had had the chance to observe me, and I was even invited to try the food prisoners were serving and, more personally, to see what a cell was like by a prisoner, showing the importance of the human side of the research process, particularly within the prison setting.

---

[1] Imprisonment for Public Protection—a sentence introduced in the Criminal Justice Act 2003 and abolished in the Legal Aid, Sentencing and Punishment of Offenders Act 2012. It is similar to a life sentence, in that it is indeterminate in length and requires the judgment of a parole board, but is in place for specified serious violent and sexual offences, and the individual can apply to have their licence conditions removed after a ten-year period following release.

[2] Offender Management Unit.

I didn't realise it at the time, but I was entering the realm of prison ethnography.

Prison Ethnography

It is arguable that this research falls into the ethnographic tradition, as the combination of interviewing, observing, and spending time within the institution gives a much deeper view of the social state of the prison as compared to the use of any of these methods individually. That said, I would contend that—if we subscribe to Bryman's concept of ethnography as entailing 'the extended involvement of the researcher in the social life of those he or she studies' (2004: 291)—the fact that the researcher could never really become involved in any extended manner in the social life of the prisoners under examination as a consequence of considerations of gender, personal safety, and relative freedom, has the result of somewhat excluding the research from the traditional field of ethnography. In addition, only a limited amount of time was spent in periods of observation on the wings and in other areas compared to time spent assisting the OMU/psychology department, simply experiencing the prison setting, taking 'advantage of whatever opportunities for observation present themselves and then to ask questions about what one has seen' (King 2000: 305), or undertaking interviews. Yet, the current definition of prison ethnography is much more flexible, and has undergone a veritable 'boom' during the period in which this book was written, with the combination of a dedicated symposium[3], and a special edition of the journal *Qualitative Inquiry*,[4] edited by Professor Yvonne Jewkes and culminating in the *Palgrave Handbook of Prison Ethnography* (2015) being published, in which the discipline is defined as:

> a form of in-depth study that includes the systematic and impressionistic recording of human cultural and social life in situ. It includes observing and/or interacting with people as they go about their everyday lives, routines and practices. We contrast an ethnographic approach with purely

---

[3] This was hosted by the International Centre for Comparative Criminological Research at the Open University and was entitled 'Resisting the Eclipse'.

[4] Qualitative Inquiry (2014), Volume 20.

interview-based research methodologies that tend to be episodic, short-lived and often take place outside of spaces the informant routinely occupies. In addition, we also recognise an ethnographic approach in commitments to the generation of 'thick' descriptive accounts of the research, though these may vary considerably in 'thickness', depth and texture. (Drake et al. 2015: 3)

Such thick descriptions became more prevalent and useful when incorporating gendered researcher reflections.

The Reflective Process

Reflection is recognised to be a crucial process in many disciplines, yet the privileging of such reflexive accounts is shied away from in much written research. In prisons, prisoners, staff, and management must constantly reflect upon their actions in order to advance—it is a key element in the majority of offending behaviour programmes that prisoners often have to engage with as part of their sentence plans. The visiting researcher should be no different. Schön, in encouraging professional reflection in and on action, makes the point that:

> when we go about the spontaneous, intuitive performance of the actions of everyday life, we show ourselves to be knowledgeable in a special way. Often we cannot say what it is that we know. When we try to describe it we find ourselves at a loss, or we produce descriptions that are obviously inappropriate. Our knowledge is ordinarily tacit, implicit in our patterns of action and in our feel for the stuff with which we are dealing. It seems right to say that our knowing is *in* action. (Schön 1983: 49)

This situation is the same for everyone—we all know different elements of life in different ways. The subjectivity of the lived experience is unavoidable, even if we wished to live some other way. What is vital, however, is the personal acknowledgement of such internalised subjectivities, in an effort for those reading your work to be able to see the research and its interpretations through the writer's eyes. The reflective notes within each substantive chapter aim to provide this viewpoint for the reader. Not only this, but as Jewkes (2012) has recognised, it allows those following in the researcher's footsteps to see the process as it really was (as opposed to the sanitised, 'happy-go-lucky' versions so often published).

For example, once in the prison, as I spent more and more time there, I began to experience the negative effects of being in such an environment—feelings of stress, empathy for prisoners that resulted in emotions, and so on. By taking notes on these feelings with my observations, the field notes turned into a reflexive diary that would be of use later in adding depth to the interview data, in addition to becoming a manner through which to purge myself of (some) emotions and stresses, and thus a way of debriefing in confidence to 'someone' who would not become overburdened by my experiences. In this research, issues surrounding the positioning of the researcher in relation to the participant and consideration of my role in shaping the knowledge that emerged were the most pertinent.

This *matters* in gendered prison research. Many of the early prison sociological studies were undertaken by men about men, but did not acknowledge this fact. If they had been more reflexive in this regard, perhaps their research could have been subjected to greater scrutiny— on the one hand, the male gender allowed these individuals access to the male social sphere within the prison, but one could question what this prevented them from seeing or hearing. How did the fact that both participants and researchers in these studies were men impact upon the interpretations made of the prison social setting, particularly when one considers the fact that the shared masculine cultural script may have left some 'normal' masculine behaviours and activities unexamined? By considering the standpoint of the researcher in a process of reflexivity, extra dimensions of the research open up. This is why reflexivity is of particular importance, particularly in prison research where the setting is generally closed off to the public eye—the manner in which interpretations are made may have wider implications as fewer others are able to scrutinise the conclusions drawn due to the relative lack of comparable knowledge, highlighting the reflexive interdependence of researcher, method, and analysis (Piacentini 2007: 155).

In this research, the research diary emerged as an extremely useful addition to the interview data, supplementing the transcripts and observations more than I had ever imagined, creating a new layer of interpretation with regard to the role of the researcher in the creation and manipulation of the research setting (a process that is regularly acknowledged in constructivist accounts), but also how the research setting can have impacts upon the researcher, which in turn shapes the outcome of the research process. It was an attempt to examine the impact on the research of the 'baggage' (Arendell 1997: 343) of those involved in the interview. I had always realised that my presence in the prison and as a researcher would shape the outcome of the research, but had never considered the possibility of the research and the prison/prisoners/staff shaping me and my personal identity/individuality. The research diary as a method of 'emotional attentiveness' (Piacentini 2007: 153) and a record was highly worthwhile and valuable—it allowed a deeper understanding of my role in the formation and interpretation of data, and from which to begin considerations as to the minimisation and relevance of the influence of subjectivities in the wider theoretical and empirical setting. My diary recorded observed interactions, my emotions, stresses, and apprehensions, and my concerns about the impact I was having upon the research.

Jewkes argues that '"wearing a mask" is arguably the most common strategy for coping with the rigours of imprisonment' (2005: 53)—the reflexive diary enabled some investigation of the nature of *the mask worn by the researcher* and, of course, the researcher's own identity in the research context. Arguably it is key not to detract from the overall focus upon the prisoner experience by undertaking 'self-indulgent navel-gazing' (Cunliffe 2003: 990), yet at the same time, as Liebling noted, 'it is impossible to be neutral. Personal and political sympathies contaminate (or less judgmentally, inform) our research' (2001: 472). As such, it is essential to recognise one's 'subjective positioning' and personal feelings regarding the research prior to its actual commencement, but it is also a useful process as it allows some recognition of the 'multiple places to stand in the story' and the 'multiple levels of emotionality' (Piacentini 2007: 163) of the researcher.

I came to this research project with little practical experience of all-male institutions, with no direct experience of researching or interviewing individuals on such a scale, particularly within the prison institution. Such feelings of wishing to help rather than hinder, and my apparent naivety, could have put me at risk when interacting with the prison population, though in practice actually seemed to be of benefit. King and Liebling state the rule: don't 'continue once compassion fatigue sets in' (2008: 445). I did not, and I am still highly sensitive to the emotional aspect of imprisonment. Yet, as Warr notes, 'it is possible to have an empathetic understanding of other people's experiences through research' (2004: 578), which may even be 'a significant guide to or even source of valuable data' (Liebling 1999: 147). Although I did my best to encourage trust and rapport with individuals, I could not justify risking my personal safety by entering into a reciprocal relationship with regard to the exchange of personal information, but by maintaining a professional and friendly, albeit private identity, it is hoped that participants were put at ease in the interview process.

The Individual, the Social, and the Researcher

The research was primarily aimed at gathering information regarding the prisoner experience, both on an individual male level, and in a collective sense, allowing a broad view of incarcerated masculinity to be observed. In addition to this, however, through the keeping of the research diary over the course of the fieldwork, it soon became apparent that a female researcher could add an extra dimension by providing the juxtapositional and relational aspect that is inherent to gendered identity (Connell 2005). These three elements of identity provide insights into the interpretation of each other.[5]

The Female Researcher

My history prior to the research provided me with a number of experiences that gave me a wide interpretative perspective when approaching the

---

[5] Yet this should be differentiated from the current trend of psychosocial research into masculinities (Gadd and Jefferson 2007), which tends to focus overly on the psychology of the individual in comparison to the social, and, most crucially, tends to leave out the role of the researcher in imposing such interpretations of psychology.

fieldwork. An only child, born in the UK, I spent a number of years of my childhood in the Middle East, usually based in (White, Western) ex-pat communities, but interacting with and learning from a wide variety of cultures. When undertaking a law degree at the University of Manchester, I lived in an all-girls hall of residence for three years, which gave me a degree of insight into single-sexed settings—albeit female and open. In addition to my MA training in International Criminology, I had a reasonably wide variety of informal experiences of the criminal justice system, shadowing police officers, solicitors, and barristers, and visiting female and male prisons to widen my knowledge prior to undertaking doctoral research. I also volunteered at a centre giving refreshments, lunch, and company to vulnerable and homeless people, in part to enhance my confidence and interpersonal skills before I entered the research site. I tried to prepare myself for what was to come. When entering the prison, I was 24.

I struggled. The prison as an institution of punishment has had a severe and long-lasting impact upon my identity as a criminologist, as a researcher, and as a woman, shaping who I was, how I behaved, and who I have since become. Not only did it alter my theoretical views regarding criminal justice and penal systems, as well as the nature of punishment and prisoners as a group, but it changed who I felt that I was on both a short- and long-term basis. I became highly security conscious both in the prison and in my home life, and found the responsibility of having a set of keys in the prison very troubling, particularly when their presence emphasised the power imbalance present between me and the research participants. I often felt highly emotional when returning prisoners to the general prison area after an interview. In addition, I suffered mood swings, had many periods of tearfulness, felt utterly exhausted, and even ended up dreaming about the prison.[6]

When actually undertaking the research, I felt the need to change who I was, particularly with reference to my gendered self—somewhat akin to the 'fronting' and mask-wearing process undertaken by prisoners themselves:

Interesting that one of my questions is about being yourself in the prison—can I be me? I have to dress differently, smell different, wear different jewellery, have

---

[6] Such experiences are not that unusual—see Liebling 1999; and Drake and Harvey 2014.

toned down hair, not for any written or spoken reason, but because I feel I should, so as to reduce my femininity in a place where it could potentially cause problems, and so that I don't stand out as an outsider (to prisoners I will by the fact that I am female, but to staff, I could just blend in—is that a good idea?). Attempting to be neutral—neither/both staff and outsider. All a matter of interpretation on the part of the observer, which I can do nothing about! (Research Diary 1, June 2009)

This had implications for my very identity, which I felt I had 'lost' when in the prison:

I don't belong here—no group affiliations, just me with everyone trying to help, but with their own groups and jobs. Can never truly fit in, as there is no single position for me to fit in to, and certainly no position of respect. Plus everyone not in psychology thinks I'm part of that group, except for the people in psychology who know and see me as something different. (Research Diary 2, June 2009)

Even trying to maintain a professional researcher identity had its problems—the stress of the setting combined with the need for a strong and proficient appearance created tensions:

Don't want to say about stress when inside—would be complaining and make me seem incompetent/incapable/not a good person to be doing the work. (Research Diary 1, June 2009)

The fact that I 'lost' my identity to a degree (even though I attempted to reclaim it part way through the fieldwork through changing my hair colour[7]) made coping with the prison environment and the emotional aspects of being in such an institution even more troublesome. I found the whole process very difficult to cope with, a fact that I had managed to forget to a degree until I reread my research diaries and revisited the depressed and stressed state that I had found myself in during the process:

I'm amazed at how emotional I get thinking about all this—but I'm encouraged too—it means I do care about people here, I do care about humanity and how men feel and are treated. I have not become desensitised, and I am starting

---

[7] Those that have met me know that I tend to opt for quite 'visible' hair colours; when in the prison, I tried to be as invisible as possible.

to look, with both eyes open, at how prisons function—so many people just see them as buildings with bad people inside, and don't think any more about it, when it is so important that they do! If we, society, the general public, sanction the state to punish people who breach societal norms and codes of convention, then we must also take on some responsibilities ourselves. (Research Diary 1, June 2009)

Both my identity as a researcher and as an individual changed over the course of the fieldwork:

Feel very much like a different me […] Aged. Feel mentally older and more thoughtful—life is much more serious. But, at the same time, I recognise the need not to take life too seriously—unsustainable for work in a prison setting. (Research Diary 3, August 2009)

Such effects, in turn, will have had implications for the research and my approach towards prisoners. In particular, I recall one incident with a prisoner which, looking back on it now, appears nowhere near as bad as I perceived it to be at the time when immersed in the situation. On one of the wings, a prisoner who I had previously spoken to expressed an interest in being interviewed. In a prior interaction, this prisoner had voiced his doubts regarding the research, appearing angry that such work would make little difference and stating—probably quite rightly—*'It's all for you'* (Research Diary 2, July 2009). The individual proceeded to give me a name and prisoner number so that I could contact him to arrange a session. After giving his details in front of other prisoners, his 'audience' then started to laugh. Upon talking to the wing's prison officers, I discovered that this prisoner had given me someone else's name and number—his reaction to my checking on his identity resulted in his exclamation of *'you snitched on me!'* (Research Diary 2, July 2009). This incident, albeit very tame, shocked me somewhat. Thus far in the process, I had not encountered any prisoners who saw me in a negative light or did not treat me with some indifference, caution, or respect, yet this prisoner felt able to mock and manipulate me in front of others. This culminated in his making a further joke to/of me in front of other prisoners regarding my need to make sure that I had checked the gate was locked behind me (this was a particular concern of mine, and appears to be where the stress and responsibility of the prison setting manifested itself most in my behaviours):

'Don't forget to lock the door, Miss.' Laughs lots when I check it.
(Research Diary 2, July 2009)

The whole thing stuck with me, raising a number of issues regarding the interactive nature of the research setting and the researcher. Not only did the incident have implications for me, but I clearly had an impact upon the prisoner and the research site by being a tool through which this individual was able to perform an identity of masculinity through his manipulation and control of my behaviours. I felt very much as if I had lost control over the situation, which frightened me—albeit only a minor joke, it highlighted the way that some prisoners could have the potential to be harmful to me. This caused me to reflect upon whether or not I should also take on the concept of a 'front' in order to protect myself (although, in reality, I already had—I just had not recognised the fact at the time):

Feel cross, angry, upset, violated, victimised, weak—playing with me in front of others. But I can leave—felt better walking out through gates and away. Embarrassed that they can mess with me, but glad I checked and followed my intuition. Very sad that they have to act in front of others—on his own he had been quite pleasant—I should not put on a front—being myself has so many advantages (especially friendly and trusting, although vigilant and checking). Just think of it as good research.[8] (Research Diary 2, July 2009)

This notion of affecting prisoners' performances of their male selves through my presence as a female non-staff member was visible on other occasions, which I interpreted in a much less threatening manner, particularly with reference to their heterosexual identities. I was used as a mechanism for verbal demonstrations of sexuality in front of others on a number of occasions. On one occasion, I was on a wing during a lunch period, talking to prisoners about the research in front of a long queue of other inmates, when a number of comments with clear sexual connotations were loudly proclaimed by various men in what was plainly a performance intended for the audience in the queue:

---

[8] I implore new prison researchers to view any negative or stressful experiences in this way!

'You should do him, Miss, he's really good'
'Can I bring some research with me?'
'Can I do some research with you?'
'You can slip your number under my door'
(Research Diary 2, July 2009)

One prisoner in particular was an excellent example of the use of my femininity as a means through which to perform his masculinity *for the benefit of others*. This individual asserted his masculinity through asking me for numbers of girls who he could call, asking about the ring that I was wearing (the implication being an inquiry into my marital status), and generally exerting a strutting and flirtatious manner in front of others. When interacting with me without such an audience, however, this individual was serious, well spoken, deferential, and respectful—he was a true pleasure to talk to. As such, I was used as a performative mechanism for masculine identity that enhanced his masculine visibility to other men. This may well have been due to the fact that I spent more time down on this wing, and thus more prisoners got to know me and felt some connection to me (and knew that I would tolerate such innuendo). Prisoners sometimes referred to me in phrases attributing some element of ownership, such as *'It's our Jenny'* (Research Diary 2, July 2009) or *'talking to my girl'* (Research Diary 3, September 2009). That said, it should also be recognised that such performances may well have had greater implications and reach on this wing, (which held a number of 'vulnerable' prisoners), as a result of the demasculinising implications of the label of vulnerability that was applied to half the men residing there.

Such a reflexive account can only go some way to showing the reciprocal effects of the research upon my individual identity, and vice versa, and even then the implications are limited to particular manifestations within me—many others would react and interpret such events and interactions differently. What it does raise, however, is the fact that prison is a hard setting and has implications for individuals' gendered selves in some form or another. If I, as a visiting researcher with keys with the ability to leave the site at any time and return to the 'real' world and the support network I had waiting for me on the outside (I lived at my parents' home, closer to the prison than mine, for the duration of the research), suffered and was affected in this way and for a prolonged period after (it took me quite a few months to feel 'normal' and 'myself' again), then this certainly raises issues regarding the hardship, stress, and emotional and mental states of those immersed within the prison for longer periods, such as staff and, in particular, individual prisoners.

The Individual Prisoner[9]

Individual prisoners, with their distinctive biographies and identities, were shaped by the prison in different ways. Some spoke of the ways that they found to cope with their predicament, such as relying upon family members outside, tailoring their personal space, or manipulating their own bodies through the gym, self-harm, or even the use of drugs. Connections to the outside world through families and (less often) friends, in addition to symbolic markers of the outside world such as decorations in the cell or upon the body, provided individuals with reminders and links to their non-prisoner identity. Through these links, and with the symbolic indicators of individuality such as taking ownership of time, space, and interactions within the jail, prisoners were able to distinguish themselves from other prisoners who they saw to be lesser men—men distinguished themselves from those who had committed particularly negatively perceived offences, and some distanced themselves from the 'dirty other' in the prison (prison thieves, drug addicts, literally dirty people, etc.). Such distinctions and assertions of individuality, often made for the benefit of the researcher during interviews (being the valued audience at that time), allowed men to position themselves within the symbolic hierarchy of the collective in a positive fashion. Men would place themselves as better than those who were 'weak' or unmanly, and

---

[9] Pseudonyms have been used to identify individuals within the text—these are completely randomly selected and are in no way related or connected to the actual participants. Using pseudonyms is merely a process whereby (a) methodological rigour can be assured through the differentiation of speakers, thereby confirming that a range of men contributed to the conclusions drawn; and (b) the men are provided with an identity (albeit unconnected to their real identities for the preservation of confidentiality) so as to show that they are individuals and not merely 'just a number'.

this was accompanied with increased personal visibility, as well as show-ing how men tried to take control over who they were *seen* to be.

As a collective body, 'prisoners' appear to be somewhat frightening. When walking around the prison, particularly during busy times such as prison movements,[10] the atmosphere was very different from one-to-one sessions with prisoners, and the prisoner collective felt somewhat indis-tinguishable, as one research diary extract shows:

> *Arrived during moves—like jumping in to a river of people all talking to each other.* (Research Diary 1, June 2009)

Devoid of any shared context other than being criminal men, such men can hardly fail to be perceived negatively or of some degree of risk. When humanised through individualisation, however, the risk of the col-lective is mitigated through the contextualisation of prisoners, their pasts, and their criminality. Their dangerousness still remains, but in some cases this is mitigated by the empathy that accompanies their histories leading up to—and within—the prison, as well as the justifications individuals gave for their experiences (and, by extension, their relative masculine positionings). As such, not only do individuals shape the nature of the collective in terms of the imported values and expectations that are com-bined, but the individual can shape the collective on a symbolic level too—not least by being a member of the audience to other men's gen-dered performances.

The Prisoner Collective

As has been seen, the presence of the female researcher had implica-tions for the prisoner collective in terms of its position as an audience for individual acts of masculine performance. In addition, however, the prisoner collective provided individual prisoners with behavioural and other gendered norms and expectations that could be used to demon-strate masculine proficiency. This is done through the symbolic force

---

[10] The periods of time when men were moved between their wings, work, healthcare, education, and so on at prescribed times of the day.

of the male gaze of other prisoners upon the individual—in fact, such gendered expectations are rarely openly expressed by members of the collective to others, but instead are anticipated, internalised, and generally self-policed by individuals who fear repercussions from failure to achieve masculine status:

Kai: Do you know what I mean it's hard to go, you can go to certain individuals I think and say, you know this is how I'm feeling, what do you think I should do about this, and they turn round and laugh at you, what you fucking talking about ei? You're your own man, do it this way or do it that way, you know it's not like…it's totally different to, to a therapeutic environment where you can go to anybody in that environment and say this is how I'm feeling, this is what's going through me head, what do you think I should be doing? And they'll offer you support in, in a proper way but here you can't, you're just seen as a weak person if you did that here, do you know what I mean

Such policing is highly dependent upon which audience actually matters and imposes policing credentials that the individual may wish to act upon. Only in extreme cases will individuals' gendered failures be physically policed, such as in the punishment of crimes that can be seen to undermine masculine values (such as sexual offences, particularly against vulnerable victims like children who men see as in need of [masculine] protection), or in the cases where one individual's failure to act according to masculine norms could result in another being seen as weak by association (such as where an individual fails to pay his debts to another prisoner, thereby requiring some form of punishment so that the dominance of the lender is assured and proven for the view of others). As such, it is the internalised collective gaze that shapes individual norms and actions—the threat of being reprimanded and rejected by the collective through which a shared identity and element of protection is established, and acting up to perceived expectations of masculinity as a coping strategy to enhance personal visibility to those who matter most to that man at that particular point in time in his life.

The triangulation of these three elements of the research gives particular insight into the nature of gendered identities as performed for the benefit of others in order to protect the self. Both the individual prisoner and the prisoner collective shaped the researcher's gendered identity—the individual through interaction and manipulation and the collective through the research-er's pre-emptive gendered and gender-led actions and interactive behaviours and expectations. The researcher, as a female, impacted upon individual pris-oners in their gendered performances for the benefit of the collective of males they needed to survive within. The researcher also affected the collective male population by providing a heteronormative spectacle for (and spectator of) masculine identity performances. Individual prisoners act in public spaces for the benefit of other prisoners' collective gendered expectations, which actu-ally emanate from, and are internalised by, individuals themselves rather than being regularly policed by the prisoner group. The individual acts for, sym-bolically creates, and is in turn shaped by the 'expectations' that are posited upon the collective male prisoner group. In turn, the collective feeds off the individual gendered expectations and norms that comprise it, policing those breaches of masculinity that could be seen to be harmful to the reputation of the group as 'positive' men—those who do not fulfil the general mascu-line norms of independence, self-sufficiency, hardness, protector (i.e. of the family), and so on are either physically (through violence), mentally (through threats, bullying, or intimidation), or symbolically (through distancing and the undermining of masculine identity) punished for their indiscretions. Such masculine traits clearly pervade the prison setting, running throughout the daily lives and aspirations of individual prisoners seeking to achieve mas-culine status, as will be seen in the following chapters.

Such a triangulation not only addresses the issues around the male prison experience and the interactions experienced (and observed) between pris-oners within the prison context, but also highlights the gendered nature of the prison context and the manners in which gendered identities (both of the male prisoner[s] and the female researcher) are performed and policed according to the particular audience, which itself has a highly gendered dimension. In addition to gender, 'race, class, and age' (Schwalbe and Wolkomir 2001: 91), and non-prisoner/prison staff status may also have played a part in the determination of the audience available for the gen-dered performance (see also Gadd and Jefferson 2007), yet these can also hide the masculinities at the very heart of offending, or the place of offend-ing in the construction of masculinities. Performances occur throughout the male population, transcending the majority of demographic variables and differentials; rather, they are shaped by who the individual man sees to be the audience that matters most to him, and that audience's expectations.

Summary

Prison research is not an easy task to undertake, both in terms of the practicalities of research within a closed-off and highly security-conscious institution, and on an emotional level, where notions of control, disempowerment, and harm are present and highly visible. My mother once said to me that she would much rather I was researching daffodils or butterflies. Yet undertaking prison research, and particularly prison ethnography, gives an insight into the human condition—in this instance from a gendered perspective. They are highly personal (and gendered) spaces, and so some consideration of the researcher's self does need to be considered, as it will undoubtedly affect the manner in which observations are interpreted and interviews are understood, and even what can or cannot be 'seen'. Sykes' (1958) pains of imprisonment, drummed into every student of prisons and penology, are highly personal pains. As such, it is important that the 'personal'—from every perspective—is brought back into the prison research project, and that we do not shy away from the emotions that accompany the process: as Jewkes (2012) states, this is doing the prison researchers of the future a huge disservice.

References

Arendell, T. (1997). Reflections on the researcher-researched relationship: A woman interviewing men. *Qualitative Sociology, 20*(3), 341–367.

Bryman, A. (2004). *Social research methods* (2nd ed.). Oxford and New York: Oxford University Press.

Connell, R. W. (2005). *Masculinities* (2nd ed.). Cambridge: Polity Press.

Crewe, B. (2005). Codes and conventions: The terms and conditions of contemporary inmate values. In A. Liebling & S. Maruna (Eds.), *The effects of imprisonment*. Cullompton: Willan Publishing.

Cunliffe, A. (2003). Reflexive inquiry in organizational research: Questions and possibilities. *Human Relations, 56*(8), 983–1003.

Drake, D. H., Earle, R., & Sloan, J. (2015). General introduction: What ethnography tells us about prisons and what prisons tell us about ethnography. In D. H. Drake, R. Earle, & J. Sloan (Eds.), *The Palgrave handbook of prison ethnography*. Basingstoke: Palgrave Macmillan.

Drake, D.H. and Harvey, J., 2014. Performing the role of ethnographer: processing and managing the emotional dimensions of prison research. *International Journal of Social Research Methodology, 17*(5), pp.489–501.

Gadd, D., & Jefferson, T. (2007). *Psychosocial criminology: An introduction.* London, Thousand Oaks, New Delhi, Singapore: Sage Publications Ltd.

Hsu, H.-F. (2005). The patterns of masculinity in prison sociology: A case study in one Taiwanese prison. *Critical Criminology, 13*, 1–16.

Jewkes, Y. (2005). Men behind bars: "Doing" masculinity as an adaptation to imprisonment. *Men and Masculinities, 8*, 44–63.

Jewkes, Y. (2012). Autoethnography and emotion as intellectual resources doing prison research differently. *Qualitative Inquiry, 18*(1), 63–75.

King, R. D. (2000). Doing research in prisons. In R. D. King & E. Wincup (Eds.), *Doing research on crime and justice.* Oxford and New York: Oxford University Press.

King, R. D., & Liebling, A. (2008). Doing research in prisons. In R. D. King & E. Wincup (Eds.), *Doing research on crime and justice* (2nd ed.). Oxford and New York: Oxford University Press.

Liebling, A. (1999). Doing research in prison: Breaking the silence. *Theoretical Criminology, 3*(2), 147–173.

Liebling, A. (2001). Whose side are we on? Theory, practice and allegiances in prisons research. *British Journal of Criminology, 41*, 472–484.

Newton, C. (1994). Gender theory and prison sociology: Using theories of masculinities to interpret the sociology of prisons for men. *The Howard Journal, 33*(3), 193–202.

Phillips, C., & Earle, R. (2010). Reading difference differently? Identity, epistemology and prison ethnography. *British Journal of Criminology, 50*(2), 360–378.

Piacentini, L. (2007). Researching Russian prisons: a consideration of new and established methodologies in prison research. In Y. Jewkes (Ed.), *Handbook on prisons.* Cullompton: Willan Publishing.

Sabo, D., Kupers, T. A., & London, W. (2001). Gender and the politics of punishment. In D. Sabo, T. A. Kupers, & W. London (Eds.), *Prison masculinities.* Philadelphia: Temple University Press.

Schon, D. A. (1983). *The reflective practitioner: How professionals think in action.* Aldershot, Brookfield USA, Singapore, Sydney: Ashgate.

Schwalbe, M., & Wolkomir, M. (2001). The masculine self as problem and resource in interview studies of men. *Men and Masculinities, 4*(1), 90–103.

Sykes, G. (1958). *The society of captives: A study of a maximum security prison* (2007th ed.). Princeton, NJ: Princeton University Press.

Warr, D. J. (2004). Stories in the flesh and voices in the head: Reflections on the context and impact of research with disadvantaged populations. *Qualitative Health Research, 14*(4), 578–587.

3

Corporeal Masculinities

Men's prisons have a very distinctive smell. The number of male bodies, doing male things, presenting male identities—corporeal masculinities—results in a very unique scent. The concept of gendered identity being an action, a presentation, a 'process' (Jenkins 2008), is particularly useful when placing the prison individual into an academic framework which argues that masculinity is also a selection of actions and processes undertaken for the benefit of both the self and others who are watching. What should be recognised from the start, however, is that this process of watching and being watched—the notion of gaze and spectacle—is highly gendered in itself. In modern Western culture, women are posited in the realm of the watched, the spectacle, the observed—men are the watchers, the spectators, the powerful gaze (see Cohan 1993; Neale 1993; Healey 1994; Boscagli 1996; White 2007: 33). Those who watch have power over the watched—the power to judge, the power to assign cultural importance through recognition, the power to grant masculinity (Kimmel 1994). With this in mind, the performance of identity is gendered before the action even begins, and the audience can be vital in shaping the process.

© The Editor(s) (if applicable) and The Author(s) 2016
J.A. Sloan, *Masculinities and the Adult Male Prison Experience*,
DOI 10.1057/978-1-137-39915-1_3

Identity is 'rooted in language', which includes 'acts, gestures, enactments' (Butler 1990: 173) but also dress, corporeal control, and even habits. This book is concerned with the male prison experience, and many participants spoke about issues and concepts that were central to their identities and the criminal and prison contexts of their lives. Although the subject of the prisoner identity has been considered for many years by those seen as the 'founding fathers' of prison studies (Clemmer, Sykes, Goffman, Irwin and Cressey, etc.), it is only a relatively recent development for such studies to give direct attention to male gendered dimensions. This book aims, in part, to see (a) how men manage their identities in an arena that arguably objectifies them, and (b) whether and how the hegemonic masculinity expectations set by the hypermasculine prison environment—and thus imposing a masculine gaze upon their states of self—makes men look at themselves as men.

The concept of the masculine corporeal identity of the participant in this research context relates to their personal selves: their prisoner and non-prisoner identities and how they used their bodies and 'performed' these as gendered individuals (as Butler [1990] and West and Zimmerman [1987] would describe it). In addition, aspects relating to who they were as criminals/prisoners *and* who they were on the outside (in addition to those factors that transcended both situations) were of interest. For example, many participants spoke in terms of how they performed their masculine identities (or how they felt that they did not) through the development of a performed front (see Crewe 2009, who also discusses the concept of 'fronting' and the use of 'masks' within prison). Managed identities were displayed *through* the body (with masculine behaviours), *by* the body (in terms of stature and poise), and *on* the body (through physical size and build, hairstyles, clothing, and so on). This chapter focuses closely on how men see themselves as men, how they see others, and how they think they may be seen through their bodies.

Male Bodies and the Prison Estate

There has been much acknowledgement of the negative implications of incarceration with regard to the female body—personal hygiene and privacy with regard to menstruation (Anderson 2009, Smith 2009), the privacy of women in front of male officers, and the maternal body of those women pre- and/or post-childbirth (Walker et al. 2014) have been used by many to differentiate women from men in prison. Yet male bodies are also affected by the prison experience. Men that I have spoken to in prison have noted the negative implications of incarceration on maintaining a positive body image, the pressures placed upon them by themselves and others to work out at the gym and supplement their diet for muscle growth, and the implications of prison time with regard to future virility and potential fatherhood (see also Phillips 2012). Former prisoners note the implications of prison with regard to men's sexual bodies (for example, masturbation—see Carcedo et al. 2015), and the problem of prison rape in male institutions is becoming more and more well known across the globe. Male and female bodies may be different, but prison clearly impacts and is framed by the bodies of those it incarcerates.

Yet, the experiences of men and women are substantially different—both in and out of prisons, men and women's bodies are viewed and used very differently according to the gendered nature of that body. In reality, women's bodies are generally the spectacle (which also explains why their bodies are foregrounded in corporeal discussions of incarceration), with men the spectators. This creates problems when individuals are placed into single-sexed institutions where there is less differentiation amongst bodies, greater proximity and competition between bodies, and much more time to contemplate the body. Men become both spectators and spectacle, thus disrupting the gendered nature of how the body is 'seen' and repositioning some men into the realm of the feminine (see also Cohan 1993). The pressures placed upon the male body are rarely acknowledged within discourse, but can have severe implications for men's interactions within the prison, and for their sense of self.

The notion of the male body being in a conflicting situation has been noted; White argues that:

the idealized male body needs to be understood as occupying an impossible space, essentially trapped between an emphasis on the exposed body as a spectacle of masculine virility and the need to repress any pleasure, desire, or eroticism associated with this subject position as the object of the admiring gaze. (2007: 22)

Although this is argued in the context of the male body on the beach, the point is clearly extendable to the prison context, where the display of masculine corporeality is of high importance as a mechanism through which to communicate male identity and meanings (Butler 1990; Sabo 2001: 65; Jewkes 2005: 58). The (physicalised) culture of masculinity has also been noted in numerous accounts; Sykes and Messinger note the importance of behaviours indicative of virility (1960: 17); Scraton et al. argue that there is a pervasive culture of masculinity within the prison, seen to reinforce hierarchies of physical dominance (1991: 66) and sustain violent acts; and Bandyopadhyay similarly notes the valorisation of influence and physical strength (2006: 190). Such a cultural emphasis upon the physical embodiment of masculine culture may explain why Thurston argues that prisons are 'centres of excellence...for the manufacture of such violent versions of masculinity' (1996: 139; see also Ricciardelli et al. 2015).

In prison, building up muscles and displays of strength show virility, as do illegitimate displays of male corporeal power such as violence and sexual offences. These are always in balance with the tensions and dangers associated with displays of homoeroticism in such a hypermasculine sphere, where display is for a male-only audience rather than in a heterosexual non-prison context where the male gaze is generally reserved for the feminine spectacle (again, see Cohan 1993; Neale 1993; Healey 1994; Boscagli 1996; White 2007: 33). Within the prison, feminine presence is often lacking, and female uniformed staff wear desexing uniforms in tandem with their male colleagues, and other non-uniformed female staff tend to be segregated from prisoners in general, only being accessible to a few by appointment for specific reasons such as treatment, sentence planning, or the use of OMU facilities. In this context, male display takes on a different meaning. Jewkes notes that 'the serious pursuit of an excessively muscular physique is significant in terms of the presentation of self as a powerful and self-controlled individual' (2002: 19). When referring to their bodies, many men spoke of the relevance of individuals' physical sizes, generally relative to others and often in relation to the amount of time they had been in prison:

Harrison: I tend to work out with the bigger men that have been in for years as well coz they seem to push you more, d'you know what I mean [...]

And there's some big people in here as well [...] (Laughs) Yeah. Some big men in here man. Coz most of them have been in from six to God knows how many years, know what I mean, so that's all they've had to do basically, eat lots of carbohydrates, coz that's all they feed you in here, potato, rice, chicken, fish, that's all they really tend to give you in here

The impact of the prison upon men's bodies was recognised by numerous participants who mentioned concerns about personal health (such as the impact of prior risky behaviours), future fertility (many spoke of wanting the opportunity to have more children in the future), and the ageing body over time through the course of their sentence. Participants also spoke of the implications of the prison diet in terms of their weight gains and losses:

Joshua: I put, I put no end of weight on since I came in, in two months I've put on about eight kilos I think
Researcher: Wow, what, is that, does that matter a lot to you?
Joshua: It does, yeah, it does
Researcher: Why?
Joshua: Well, I don't like, I don't like putting on weight gain (laughs) I don't like to weigh eighty kilos, it's just not me. But I think, you know I think even though you're exercising, you're not exercising as much [...] you know... [...] Yeah, but you can only, you can only do so much in one hour, you know, and then... [...] It's not like you're walking round all day, coz you're not, you're just sat down most of the time. And then you're eating fatty foods on top

Such developments in weight from diet and exercise had implications for participants in terms of body confidence; whilst such issues tend to be associated with women, they are increasingly suffered by men (see, for example, Ricciardelli et al. 2007). Eating disorders themselves have been linked to problems concerning identity (Polivy and Herman 2002). Many spoke of the importance of being the right size (both in their own minds and through the observation of others' actions):

Researcher: And what's good about the gym?
Zachary: Um, obviously the, the effects, seeing what it does to your physique afterwards is probably the biggest incentive [...] And um, for me, I think um, going back to masculine identity again it's about being strong [...] You

Researcher: know? Even though I'm not the kind of person to…to be aggressive, out-
               wardly aggressive to other people, but it's nice to know that you're strong
Researcher: Yeah, is it reassuring?
Zachary: Um, not really reassuring, yeah I guess it is reassuring, yeah, it is…it's just
               nice, and there's something weird about it knowing that you can lift a
               certain amount of weight and it looks a bit intimidating at first and then
               you manage to get over that hurdle

Vanity played a part in many participants' daily lives, being the reason for their concerns about weight, their need to exercise, and the impact of their hair, clothing, keeping clean, and so on. A number of participants spoke of how they looked relative to other prisoners, and the bodies of other men played a part in shaping the behaviours of participants—body language was observable, and one participant in particular described how his body changed in response to being around others:

Zachary: […] I think if you walked around the wings…but they couldn't see you,
               coz if they see you then it's totally different, but if you walked, if you was
               observing unobserved then I guess you'd see people walking like muscles
               tense and I guess I do it sometimes as well subconsciously like walk
               around with my shoulders a bit higher or tensed and um, chest out, just
               being men I guess, but um…
Researcher: […] little things like that just with the way you, you actually notice your-
               self doing it?
Zachary: Yeah, it's embarrassing, I don't want to do it but it's one of those kind of
               things it's in prison it's kind of automatic now, and you do do it
Researcher: But you wouldn't do it on the outside?
Zachary: No, no, because I wouldn't feel threatened on the outside, that's why
Researcher: So do you feel threatened all the time in here then?
Zachary: Yeah, you do I guess…coz no one wants to be, it's just a harsh environment
               isn't it, it's not um…it's just uh one of those kind of…it's a place where
               you definitely, your masculine side needs to come to the forefront because
               otherwise then you will be targeted and…I guess made to like ostracised
               or made to feel inferior and people just want a…peaceful time, so I
               guess…guess that's the reason yeah. Not sure why it's got, it's got to this
               stage or why it is the way it is but…definitely that is how it is

Male bodies displayed many markers of the prisoner's life, including tattoos, piercings, smells, and, most notably, scars from prior harm, both from others and self-inflicted. In addition, men's muscles were immediate signifiers of masculinity, with a number of participants displaying for me as an audience through pointing them out and flexing (see also Phillips 2012). As Jewkes suggests:

> the constructed, laboured-over body is the locus of an under valued presence in the world, albeit one which is open to reconstruction and the pleasures of narcissism. (2002: 19)

In essence, many men spent time and effort on their bodies because they had little else practical to do (which can be quite a demoralising state to live in, especially for a prolonged period of time). The gym was a major masculine focus in the jail, with many speaking about their enjoyment of the facility, and the advantages that it brought to their bodies. In fact, it is arguable that men took so much pride in their bodies not only because it was one of the only ways in which they could perform their masculine identities or, as some did, display their removal from this system of performance and competition. It also provided men with an extra element of control over their lives through the manipulation of their corporeal selves, and an ability to express ownership over a key aspect of their masculine identities, as well as enhancing their masculine physical visibility to others.

One further manner in which individuals could add an element of meaning to their bodies was through the use of tattoos. Tattoos have been theorised as being a subcultural practice of deviation which could be indicative of personality disorders (Post 1968), whereas others have seen tattoos as a means to express identity and demonstrate toughness (Watson 1998). In the prison under study, tattoos mainly served as literal forms of communication of identity to others, inscribed upon the body. Names of children, partners, and parents commonly indicated the masculine familial position of an individual, with symbols also indicating hardness and the ability to withstand physical pain. Some originated from the prison context; however, many originated from well before this time and linked to their lives outside the prison. Although few spoke of their tattooing practices, the narratives of a few related to manners of control over time in the alleviation of boredom, or over their own bodies:

Samuel: And because of my low self esteem and…basically had hardly any self-respect for myself and I just abused my body really, most of my hands anyway. And then as I grew older I kind of got in a passion for tattooing and realised the, the respect behind it and the appreciation and ended up doing tattoos myself

Scars were also an intriguing identity signifier, as they sometimes demonstrated hardness in terms of an individual's history of being involved in violence, whereas at other times they signified vulnerability, being the result of self-harming strategies of coping. At the same time, such perceived markers of vulnerability could be tempered by the fact that they showed an individual was willing to be violent, albeit directing the violence inwardly upon their selves.

The male body within prison is, therefore, a key element in creating identity, acting as a canvas for non-verbal communication, both directly through the body and via markers placed upon that body. In addition, the body was used to position oneself relative to others in terms of size, temporal features, control, and ownership over the self. The interaction between the prison and the body was generally seen in a negative light, in terms of changing appearances due to prison food, prison time, health implications, and an overall lack of full self-governance. Issues of body confidence and vanity played out in ways that might appear feminine if not situated within discourses of toughness and physicality, and the researcher's gender was sometimes used as a means through which to masculinise such displays.

Clothing

Another way in which men are able to demonstrate masculinity upon their bodies is through clothing: Frith and Gleeson have found that clothing plays an important part in men's processes of self-surveillance and self-presentation (2004)—processes that are even more significant in prison where other means of demonstrating masculinity are unavailable and where men are constantly performing for audiences to grant them masculine credentials. Clothing did come up as a subject in participants' discussions, in addition to being observed during the course of the research. Many prisoners wore elements of the standard prison attire—a grey sweatsuit—yet often they would add an element of their own to their outfits, such as bright shoes, hats, watches, and bracelets. Some of these sent official messages, as they would be worn by people who were on the toe-to-toe scheme—where certain prisoners help others to learn to read—as an indicator that they were able to help in that way. This was the same with some shirts which indicated that individuals were Listeners (trained by the Samaritans) or on a representative committee. Such additions enhanced the visibility of these individuals' positions of respect and influence over the lives of others.

The grey sweatsuit itself highlights a compelling aspect of the prison experience, in that—certainly in this prison—the colour grey sends out a message of dullness and a lack of excitement and vitality. It is neither one thing nor another. It was noted in one of the research diaries in an observation of one of the prison movements that there were '*lots of grey tracksuits—why? A hopeless colour*' (Research Diary 1, June 2009).

The additions that many participants chose to make to their outfits often acted as signifiers in a similar manner to the outside world: participants made note of the fact that they often had to save up for clothing, and it had a distinct monetary value, therefore wearing expensive items such as branded trainers signifies some manner of wealth. As Crewe recognised, 'it is notable that white trainers, the footwear of choice in prison, are the goods most capable of displaying newness and therefore indicating income' (2009: 277). Jewkes also recognised the importance of footwear as 'one indicator of both lifestyle aspirations and the need to signal to the group something of one's preprison identity…they literally wear their masculine credentials on their feet' (2005: 57). In addition to being of monetary value, clothing was noted to be consequential in terms of participants owning their personal space—having their own clothes in their cells put their mark and identity on that space (see also Baer 2005). Clothing was seen in some cases to act as an extension of the self and the personality of the individual, such as the wearing of football shirts to signify allegiances, in the same way as it was outside. This did have its drawbacks:

Connor: … a lot of people don't like things like that because it's not the norm, they're like rather you walked round like this, you know…like a robot, and some of the clothes I wear […] they don't, they just don't like them, what's not the norm

As such, clothing being an extension of personality has the result that individuals have to police what they wear as well as how they act. In an extension of this, clothing was also used as a way to distinguish one's self from other prisoners:

Finlay: It's…I just totally, I don't want to be like them you know, the mental health nurse, she thinks I'm funny man, she goes listen you're too individual, all kinds of like bright T-shirts and things like that

How certain signifiers were seen was not always as the wearers would have intended them:

Harvey: …it's stupid, plastic gangsters (laugh) […] walking around with their trousers down to their ankles, arse showing […] Walking about they've got a stone in their shoe and ah […] Yeah, you go out there on the exercise yard you see them, loads of them, they're all standing there with their 50 Cent baseball caps, jeans down to there, uh funny, funny (laughs) fifty pence

Participants also spoke of the distinct nature of prison clothing, in that the way they dressed was often linked to their situation and the type of masculine identity they wanted to demonstrate—some spoke of dressing differently when inside prison compared to outside, and others spoke of dressing up for visits:

Freddie: …I mean I always wear prison clothes, and it's just because I feel, I feel prison's dirty, I wear my own clothes whenever I have a visit or when I've got something to, I should, I should have dressed up today for you

Clearly dress was a central dimension to the performance for particular audiences.

A number spoke similarly of the association they gave to prison through certain clothes (in effect, those clothes being a signifier of their time and identity in prison), speaking of their plans to wear different clothing on the outside (often new and thus 'untainted' by the prison identity). As such, clothing was seen to be a signifier of their situated identities, firmly positioned within the discourses of the sites that they inhabited and very much about their sense of being masculine and retaining control over their senses of self (see also Phillips 2012):

Oscar: I suppose I feel like a man outside. Where I can dress like a man. Dunno, that that, no. Don't feel like a man in here. No, not really

Controlling and Protecting the Self

Most prison researchers acknowledge a need for the specifically protective performance of the individual's displayed self within the prison for other prisoners, and this discourse is situated within a culture of 'fear' of other men. Such frontings were encountered by Crewe, who recognised that defensive presentations of the self undermined the development of trust and created a presumption of artificiality (2009: 308). As such, the 'front' is framed in a negative manner, but Jewkes discusses the fact that the wearing of a 'mask' in prison is 'arguably the most common strategy for coping with the rigors of imprisonment' (Jewkes 2005: 53).

The implication is that individuals cannot be their 'true' selves within the prison, yet this implies that men *can* be themselves elsewhere, a notion that is somewhat difficult to resolve when one recognises that gender is performed throughout our lives for the benefit of whichever audience is at hand—we act the way we want others to see us at a particular point in time, or how we want to see ourselves if alone. With this in mind, it might be more appropriate to situate the notions of 'fronting' and 'masks' within the wider Butler-esque concepts of gendered performances, and see the prison setting as having a distinct type of audience with distinct gendered powers and influence. These could equally be experienced on the outside, but are often tempered with feminine audience members or men who have less to lose within the masculine hierarchy due to its reduced hypermasculine status when outside the restrictive and containing prison walls. As such, the impact of others upon personal identities (and places and spaces) was recognised to be substantial:

Samuel: ...because I think when you're on the wing you do have to put up a certain...although I, I put up a certain guard...I, I, I still allow myself to be who I am...and, you know, and don't let it get in the way of how I conduct myself on the wing or how people see me... [...] but I still keep

myself...distanced, because, at the end of the day, I'm in jail, and anything can happen at any time (click) off it kicks. Not with me but, um...
somewhere on the wing, you know, and it's, so, so I'm always prepared for
that...so I think once I'm in my cell it's like...right, that's done for
another day...

Other prisoners similarly spoke of the ways in which they limited or
altered their identities for the benefit of certain audiences, be that in the
limitation of emotionality in the process of demonstrating masculine
toughness; in the demonstration of family values and identities when making contact with supporters outside the prison; or even in the demonstration
of certain masculine traits to or through me as a female researcher. It became
clear that gendered identities were highly flexible (my own included), highlighting the processes men undertook in drawing upon different masculine
resources that they had (both internalised and through others and spaces)
according to the varying audience at hand. Rather than seeing performance
as being a variable that can be stripped off to expose an underlying gendered essentialism or 'truth' to masculine identity (Goffman's 'backstage'
area—1958: 69), it becomes more useful to see the notion of masculine (or
gendered) performances as constant, with the demands of the audience for
such demonstrations being the variable instead:

Zachary: Coz going back to what I was saying before, um...people like to put a
           little protective bubble around themselves coz...we are in an environ-
           ment where kind of the alpha male will rule and um...people are just on
           guard in here because you don't want to be like ridiculed or humiliated
           because you can't get away, you're trapped in this environment, so I guess
           your reputation means a lot [...]

Kevin: Always have to have a front on [...] Coz you, if you're too emotional like
           if I talk to the way I talk to you to like a prisoner coz I've, I've, I've, I've
           talked to you with no boundaries [...] If I talked to someone like that
           they'd think you were an idiot [...] Way I think yeah, yeah. Have to have
           a tough image

Covering up signs of weakness with a tough front was one of the
foremost aspects of identity management for these individuals, as this
could enable them to get through the prison experience without being

victimised or bullied by the prisoner audience which was of particular influence at that time in their lives:

Researcher: So what is it, what is it that you change, I mean do you, do you just talk to people less or do you change your posture or anything?

Kai: No it's more of…your mannerisms and your aura, your aura about your-self, d'you know what I mean it's like…you, you, you won't let people see you as…as being someone who can't handle situations of you can't do this, you can't do that, I'm not saying that you have to be aggressive you don't have to be aggressive 23 hours a day or…like confrontational or owt like that but you've got to be able to show that you're willing to be a part of that

This attitude was more evident when prisoners were younger, and many said it occurred a lot in young offenders' institutions (some spoke of the fact that they had to do it much less in adult jail by comparison). In actuality, 'laddishness' in young men has been recognised to be a process through which boys are protecting their self-worth (Jackson 2002); and within the prison context, 'where physical vulnerability is salient, prisoners may be more likely to use overstated aggressive mascu-line presentations to minimize harm, which in turn perpetuates or exacerbates existing physical risks' (Ricciardelli et al. 2015: 509). This would explain the high levels of violence in such arenas where boys are already feeling challenged about their self-worth, and feel physically at risk more. It was explained, in part, as 'proving' themselves as men to the accompanying young male audience, which has key expectations of gendered performance that it imposed:

Jude: When I was a YP, young offender, um…it's that sort of…environment that you've got a lot of youngsters and everyone's kind of vying for position and I think you have to be someone else, you have to put up a sort of barrier, have to put up a…what's the word I'm looking for?…you have to put a front on, you know

So the 'front' that participants spoke of was what they wished others to see in them, and they managed behaviours and identities that were symbolic of what participants felt they 'should' be seen to be within this context. This was also done with words—participants spoke of observing many prisoners telling stories, particularly with reference to their criminal actions, their reputations outside, and their wealth, in order to try to impress and impose a sense of masculine bravado. The notion of storytelling (particularly in prison) has been recognised to be key in the process of 'the production and reproduction of particular versions or discourses of doing or accomplishing masculinity in this cultural arena' (Thurston 1996: 139—see also Jewkes 2002, 2005). Crewe recognises the notion of prison landings being 'catwalks of masculine display' (2009: 410), as implied by this individual:

Researcher: Right, ok. So how did you, what, when you say you put on a front, what did you have to do? How do you…

Benjamin: Swear a lot. Walk around, walk around like you've got two buckets of water (laughs) […] In the right places, yeah, not, not constantly but in the right places […] Swear a lot, be loud

Specific gendered performances according to different audiences occur in day-to-day life generally, but within the prison it seemed functional and much more gendered in terms of preserving the masculine self and maintaining control over who (and the kind of man) one is seen to be. This requires care, as to be seen to be too guarded can suggest an individual has something to cover up, such as an unattractive criminal conviction or fear, both leaving the participant vulnerable to harm or labels of weakness (see Chapter 7)—in this way, how visible an individual is or is not can have implications for how they are seen with regard to the gendered lens. Performances occurred for the benefit of others' views of the individual, for the benefit of the appearance of the collective prisoner group, and for the benefit of the individual prisoner himself. One manner of coping with the emasculating prison experience was clearly to perform alternative or extreme masculine behaviours—often explained as being for the benefit of the collective masculine gaze of the prison. However, when considering the limited instances of outward social policing of such gendered norms compared with the self-policing of gendered identity, such demonstrations may have had more force in reassuring the individual of his own masculine well-being, potential, and self.

Identity management was a complicated matter, where performed public identities in the prison differed from those expressed in private settings behind bars. This in turn may well have differed from individuals' identities as seen outside prison, where mechanisms to perform identity and 'do masculinity' (Messerschmidt 1993) are less restricted in terms of the ability to accrue possessions, juxtapose identities against the female gender and the family institution, and be involved in other masculine cultures such as sports, drinking, work, and autonomous behavioural choices.

Within the prison estate, participants recognised having to perform their selves differently in a higher-security prison compared to a YOI, an open prison, or a therapeutic community. Throughout the prison estate (and more so the higher the degree of security imposed), 'legitimate' resources through which to display such gendered identities were often lacking, leaving less attractive but prominent tools such as violence and threats. Participants who had already been denied legitimate means to perform their masculine identities outside of prison had even fewer such resources within, and were left with violent behaviours, expressions of dominance over others, lies about personal situations, and even theft of goods from others as 'easy' ways through which to build up personal 'wealth' and achieve what Crewe refers to as 'consumer masculinity' (2009: 277). The use of different gender resources in this way could have substantial implications for how a man was 'seen'—both by others and himself (with the two not necessarily overlapping)—in the present and in the future.

There is clearly a struggle over men's sense of self and how others might see them relative to who they 'should be' as men. Identities and bodies within prison intersect with many other themes and subthemes considered in other chapters of this book; however, although the majority of individuals focus upon the individualistic nature of their identities and the control that they personally have over who they are, they also acknowledge that this is flexible in its development over time and space (see Chapters 4 and 5), and developed relative to, and for the benefit of, a varying collection of others within the prison setting. This is done behaviourally, vocally, and physically, and amounts to a form of personal performance of self that is dependent upon the audience at hand as to which aspects of identity are highlighted or hidden. What is most fascinating perhaps is the split between how these men want to see themselves (and why and for whose benefit) and how they actually practice being men: what they choose to do with their bodies and how that relates to who they say they 'are' and to whom.

Reflexive Note

As a female researcher in a male prison, my body was one of the key elements that differentiated me from everyone else in the prison at first sight. Even though there were female staff there, not only did they tend to dress differently, but they also held themselves and performed their identities in very different ways—not least due to their pre-existing experience of working within a prison, and their symbolic control over the men, which immediately placed them as the dominant and the male prisoner as the dominated, reversing the gender norms emanating from patriarchal cultural systems. With this being a relatively new environment to me as a researcher, and this being my first piece of lone empirical research, my performed self ended up coming across as young, feminine, and naive.

One of the main corporeal considerations on my mind when entering the prison was how to dress. I tried wearing a suit for professionalism, and was interpreted to be a governor (i.e. management in the prison)—not exactly helpful when trying to get prisoners to trust you enough to tell their stories and to see you as something other than the institution. I then attempted to blend into the background and hide my femininity through wearing baggy clothes and trying not to be too 'obvious' so that I could observe the prison without being too visible. That was an epic failure. I was young, female, and clearly did not fit: evidenced in one prisoner shouting out of the window to me when I was checking that I had locked a door, that I was clearly new, I would get used to it and, when I didn't respond, the (performed) comment 'nice arse' (see also Genders and Player 1995 for discussion on female researcher dress).

In the end, my young femininity was useful, in that the men did see me as 'other' and not part of the institution (although there were some that aligned me with psychology—not a positive place to be from the prisoner perspective [see Sloan and Wright 2015])—in fact, my naivety made men want to explain things to me more, and almost take me under their wings in a protective stance.

How I acted and how I looked played on my mind a lot in the prison, and, looking back, gave me a tiny insight into how stressful and tiring it must be to have to act and perform for an audience that is potentially risky. It is exhausting, and removes the individual from who they really are—sometimes to the point of no return (Schmid and Jones 1991).

Summary

This chapter has given consideration to a broad range of aspects of the corporeal identities and contexts of prisoners on both individual and collective levels. Whereas the majority of academic discourse regarding prisoner identity tends to disregard masculinity as a central variable, analysis of the areas of relevance that emerged revealed maleness to be fundamental. The centrality of the male corporeal identity as an independent influence in individual (and collective) prisoner performances, rather than being encumbered by other variables, allows prisoner behaviours to be situated within the wider sphere of masculine demonstration. Rather than resorting to processes of fragmentation through categorisation of various identity typologies as many have done before, the use of masculinity as a single analytical lens through which to understand various forms of identity negotiation within the prison has actually had the opposite effect, bringing various different types of men in prison together in terms of the similarities in their behaviours and bodies with reference to male identity.

Performances were constantly occurring within the prison as men tried to take control over the types of men they wished to be seen as, often using literal performances of masculine signifiers drawing upon masculine signposts that transcended the prison situation, such as wealth, control (as Jewkes pointed to with reference to the body [2002: 19], and can be seen in terms of the way men used their bodies as indicators of male toughness and strength through muscles, tattoos, clothing, and so on), fatherhood, virility, work, and masculine cultural stereotypes. Prisoners can be said to perform their identities for the benefit of others—being oneself was found to be a highly elaborate matter, underpinned with requirements to undertake managed and normative behaviours, front, hide weaknesses, and prove masculinity (particularly earlier in an individual's life).

Masculine identities and their bodily signifiers were of high importance and relevance to identities and contexts within the prison sphere. The body was the key mechanism through which to demonstrate masculine self—be that how it was used to perform the gendered self, how it was mastered and defined either through muscles or markings, or how it was enrobed in costume. Yet all of these masculine processes sit in tension with the fact that such performances within the prison are generally for the benefit of other men, disrupting heteronormative conceptions of the male gaze—in other contexts such behaviours and practices would be placed within the realm of the homoerotic. Despite this tension, such aspects of corporeal masculinity were ingrained in the very essences of these individuals, and were central to their identities in the past, present, and future spheres.

References

Anderson, J. (2009). The problem of "Manhood" in a women's prison. In Gershenson, O. & Penner, B. (Eds.), *Ladies and gents: Public toilets and gender*. USA: Temple University Press.

Baer, L. D. (2005). Visual imprints on the prison landscape: A study on the decorations in prison cells. *Tijdschrift voor Economische en Sociale Geografie, 96*(2), 209–217.

Bandyopadhyay, M. (2006). Competing masculinities in a prison. *Men and Masculinities, 9*, 186–203.

Boscagli, M. (1996). *Eye on the flesh: Fashions of masculinity in the early twentieth century*. Colorado and Oxford: Westview Press Inc.

Butler, J. (1999). *Gender trouble: Feminism and the subversion of identity*. London and New York: Routledge.

Carcedo, R. J., Perlman, D., López, F., Orgaz, M. B., & Fernández-Rouco, N. (2015). The relationship between sexual satisfaction and psychological health of prison inmates the moderating effects of sexual abstinence and gender. *The Prison Journal, 95*(1), 43–65.

Cohan, S. (1993). 'Feminising' the song-and-dance man: Fred Astaire and the spectacle of masculinity in the Hollywood musical. In S. Cohan & I. R. Hark (Eds.), *Screening the male: Exploring masculinities in Hollywood cinema*. London and New York: Routlegde.

Crewe, B. (2009). *The prisoner society: Power, adaptation, and social life in an English prison*. Oxford, New York: Oxford University Press.

Frith, H., & Gleeson, K. (2004). Clothing and embodiment: Men managing body image and appearance. *Psychology of Men & Masculinity, 5*(1), 40.

Genders, E., & Player, E. (1995). *Grendon: A study of a therapeutic prison*. Oxford: Clarendon Press.

Goffman, E. (1958). *The presentation of self in everyday life*. Edinburgh: University of Edinburgh Social Sciences Research Centre. Monograph No. 2.

Healey, M. (1994). The mark of a man: Masculine identities and the art of macho drag. *Critical Quarterly, 36*(1), 86–93.

Jackson, C. (2002). 'Laddishness' as a self-worth protection strategy. *Gender and Education, 14*(1), 37–50.

Jenkins, R. (2008). *Social identity* (3rd ed.). Abingdon and New York: Routledge.

Jewkes, Y. (2002). *Captive audience: Media, masculinity and power in prisons*. Cullompton: Willan Publishing.

Jewkes, Y. (2005). Men behind bars: "Doing" masculinity as an adaptation to imprisonment. *Men and Masculinities, 8*, 44–63.

Kimmel, M. S. (1994). Masculinity as homophobia: Fear, shame, and silence in the construction of gender identity. In H. Brod & M. Kaufman (Eds.), *Theorizing masculinities*. Thousand Oaks and London: Sage.

Messerschmidt, J. W. (1993). *Masculinities and crime*. Maryland: Rowman and Littlefield Publishers, Inc.

Neale, S. (1993). Prologue: Masculinity as spectacle – Reflections on men and mainstream cinema. In S. Cohan & I. R. Hark (Eds.), *Screening the male: Exploring masculinities in Hollywood cinema*. London and New York: Routledge.

Phillips, C. (2012). *The multicultural prison: Ethnicity, masculinity and social relations among prisoners*. Oxford: Oxford University Press.

Polivy, J., & Herman, C. P. (2002). Causes of eating disorders. *Annual Review of Psychology, 53*, 187–213.

Post, R. S. (1968). Relationship of tattoos to personality disorders. *Journal of Criminal Law, Criminology and Police Science, 59*, 516.

Ricciardelli, R., Maier, K., & Hannah-Moffat, K. (2015). Strategic masculinities: Vulnerabilities, risk and the production of prison masculinities. *Theoretical Criminology, 19*(4), 491–513.

Ricciardelli, L. A., McCabe, M. P., Williams, R. J., & Thompson, J. K. (2007). The role of ethnicity and culture in body image and disordered eating among males. *Clinical Psychology Review, 27*, 582–606.

Sabo, D. (2001). Doing time, doing masculinity: Sports and prison. In D. Sabo, T. A. Kupers, & W. London (Eds.), *Prison masculinities*. Philadelphia: Temple University Press.

Schmid, T. J., & Jones, R. S. (1991). Suspended Identity: Identity transformation in a maximum security prison. *Symbolic Interaction, 14*(4), 415–432.

Scraton, P., Sim, J., & Skidmore, P. (1991). *Prisons under protest*. Milton Keynes: Open University Press.

Sloan, J., & Wright, S. (2015). Going in green: Reflections on the challenges of 'getting in, getting on, and getting out' for doctoral researchers. In D. H. Drake, R. Earle, & J. Sloan (Eds.), *The Palgrave handbook of prison ethnography*. Palgrave Macmillan: Basingstoke.

Smith, C. (2009). A period in custody: Menstruation and the imprisoned body. *Internet Journal of Criminology*, 1–22.

Sykes, G. M., & Messinger, S. L. (1960). The inmate social system. In R. A. Cloward (Ed.), *Theoretical studies in social organisation of the prison*. New York: Social Science Research Council.

Thurston, R. (1996). Are you sitting comfortably? Men's storytelling, masculinities, prison culture and violence. In M. Mac an Ghaill (Ed.), *Understanding masculinities: Social relations and cultural arenas*. Buckingham, UK: Open University Press.

Walker, J. R., Hilder, L., Levy, M. H., & Sullivan, E. A. (2014). Pregnancy, prison and perinatal outcomes in New South Wales, Australia: A retrospective cohort study using linked health data. *BMC Pregnancy and Childbirth, 14*(1), 214.

Watson, J. (1998). 'Why Did You Put That There?': Gender, materialism and tattoo consumption. *Advances in Consumer Research, 25*(1), 453.

West, C., & Zimmerman, D. H. (1987). Doing gender. *Gender and Society, 1*(2), 125–151.

White, C. (2007). "Save Us from the Womanly Man": The transformation of the body on the beach in Sydney, 1810 to 1910. *Men and Masculinities, 10*(1), 22–38.

4

Temporal Masculinities

Time, Imprisonment, and Masculinities

Thomas Cottle makes the highly significant point that:

> all human beings must work out their own conceptions of time flow and
> their own perceptions of the temporal horizon. They must deal with the
> historical past that existed before their births and with their own pasts,
> their own presents. They also must deal with their personal future and its
> unknowable content. (1976: 188)

When one reads this through the lens of imprisonment, such 'workings
out' that incarcerated men have to undertake become substantially more
challenging and limited by virtue of the prisoner label and how it defines
men's pasts, presents, and potential futures. It is clear that time is central
to the prison experience. The very point of imprisonment is to deprive an
individual of their liberty and autonomy—their freedom to spend their
time freely—and the length of the sentence is reflective of the serious-
ness of the crime committed. Matthews (2009: 37/38) argues that there
are four elements that can be attributed to time-centred punishment: its

© The Editor(s) (if applicable) and The Author(s) 2016
J.A. Sloan, *Masculinities and the Adult Male Prison Experience*,
DOI 10.1057/978-1-137-39915-1_4

universal and independent nature relative to the individual prisoner; its objective and solid nature compared to other forms of expressive punishment; the social quality of time-as-punishment; and the commodification of time (Giddens 1981: 130) that, as Wahidin points out, can be 'lost, gained, saved, wasted or ingeniously endured' (2006: 3.1; see also Cohen and Taylor 1972: 87).

Ministry of Justice statistics show that from 1999 to 2011 there was an increase of 1.4 months in the average time served in prison for determinate sentence prisoners, due to an increase in average custodial sentence lengths being sentenced and a decline in parole release rates (Ministry of Justice 2013: 1). The introduction of tougher sentencing policies in line with the 'Tough on Crime' agenda of the 1990s/2000s, such as the creation of Imprisonment for Public Protection[1] and mandatory minimum sentences (Crime [Sentences] Act 1997) have had the effect of increasing the time individuals serve within the prison setting. In addition, research has shown that the impact of prison as an interrupting event in an individual's life course creates concerns regarding employment, education, and the return to social lives, all of which are shaped by developments in time (Wilson 2010: 7) as well as being key signifiers of masculine identity.

Matthews (2009) argues that prisoners go through processes of the negotiation of time, either legitimately through the creation of routines, or through illegitimate means such as the taking of drugs that are 'able to place time into further suspension and thereby release the prisoner, albeit temporarily, from the apparent timelessness of prison life' (2009: 39). Although Matthews offers no evidence for this claim, his presupposition was supported by some of the comments within the research project, such as:

Logan: [...] the sentence I'm doing it's not as clear cut so I've got more time to do here and there's not really a lot of things for me to do here [...] So...it can drag a bit your time here if you don't find ways to occupy it more

Henry: If them drugs are making you feel happy in a cell of a night, and you're not getting stressed out and you're not worrying about your prison, and you're

---

[1] (Criminal Justice Act 2003, amended by the Criminal Justice and Immigration Act 2008), now abolished by the Legal Aid, Sentencing and Punishment of Offenders Act 2012, which replaced IPP with a life sentence following a second listed offence (s122).

happy in your cell out of your head, then you carry on taking drugs. If it makes your sentence easier for you then do it, d'you see what I'm saying, if you drink alcohol then drink your drink, do whatever it is that you feel necessary to get on with your sentence, don't worry about what other people think or what the authorities think, you just do what's necessary for you as a person

Perceptions of time are not only relevant for the impact of incarceration in terms of its deterrent effects—they play a key role in the shaping of identities and the general prison experience. Identities change over the life course, and so will continue to develop when in the prison environment (Medlicott 1999), yet will be shaped by events that are prison-specific, thus creating (or forcing the creation of) a prison identity (see Schmid and Jones 1991). Medlicott (1999) has noted that individuals who have been found to fail to cope with imprisonment have shown signs of the denial or distortion of such time, compared to copers who are more accepting and forward looking, highlighting the ways in which time can shape behaviours and mental coping strategies, and who men essentially *are*.

Wahidin and Tate have considered the implications of time upon the female prisoner, particularly with reference to the ageing female body, arguing time to be a constituent part in the construction of gendered identity due to the impacts regarding family, age, female bodily functions, appearance, and forms of resistance to this process (2005: 60). They argue that women experience prison time as a 'somatic identity cipher' (2005: 65) and attempt to reinscribe time through performativity. As such, they emphasise the importance female prisoners ascribe to being able to own and control time in some way, with the value of time being inherently connected to time that is 'lost'. Although this is arguably the case with those individuals who maintain a close connection with the outside world, which many women (and men) will tend to do due to their intimate identity connection with external institutions such as the family, it is arguable that this is too simplistic a definition. Time within the prison can also have a form of positive value, such as having time for personal development and treatment (Inciardi et al. 1997: 264), and the negative value of time is not only that which is equivocal with the outside—although this is key to the nature of time as discipline. Many of the points made about women inmates and ageing bodies are transferable to the male situation.

Time, Punishment, and Gender

In modern penality, the concept of time has been incorporated into the day-to-day policies involved in prisons—the Prison Rules guiding the functioning of prisons state the purpose of prison training and treatment (of convicted prisoners) to be to 'encourage and assist them to lead a good and useful life' (The Prison Rules 1999: Rule 3), thereby highlighting the importance of the positive use of an individual's time and its implications for their future. This is echoed in the HMI Prisons 'Healthy Prison' assessment, which includes the notion of purposeful activity, whereby 'prisoners are able, and expected, to engage in activity that is likely to benefit them' (HM Inspectorate of Prisons 2012: 83). With this in mind, the process of punishment is perceived in policy to be both linear—in terms of the progression of an individual through time and development—and cyclical—with respect to the consistency in day-to-day functioning across the prison system through routines and shift patterns (see Wahidin 2006: 6.19; Medlicott 2008: 293; Matthews 2009; Moran 2012).

The implications of the combination of cyclicality and linearity for prisoners has been recognised to be a central aspect of punishment with reference to the 'fracture of their psychological time consciousness' (Medlicott 2008: 293), in that the true linear nature of their outside lives, of which they are in direct control, is both unavailable and continuously attempted to be adhered to through emotions and connections to the outside world: a 'horrible mismatch of one's internal time-consciousness and the reality of prison time' (Medlicott 1999: 225). Wahidin refers to the process of disconnection with outside time systems and events as a form of 'social death' (2006: 6.11), which female prisoners would find ways to mitigate where possible. When one looks at such propositions regarding men, it is clear that there are serious implications regarding masculine identity and the lack of control over time: as this book contends, control is a key dimension of the masculine self.

The implications of the combinations of linear and cyclical time take on even greater significance when one looks closer at the gendered nature of time. As Maines and Hardesty note, 'men and women live in different temporal worlds' (1987: 102). Daly states that there is a phenomenological difference in men and women's experiences of time (1996: 145); biologically and psychologically, women tend to experience their lives in terms of cycles and rhythms, whereas men experience time in a more linear fashion, not least due to patriarchal power and status:

> societal linear time [...] is shaped by culture, technology and industrial production. Linear time is the essence of masculine experience. Work and career continue to be the most salient aspects of identity for men, which is expressed in time as progression and achievement. (Daly 1996: 145)

Odih also notes the connection between masculinity and 'linear time', in that 'linear time's continual transcendence from the present resonates with masculinity's compulsive hyperactivity' (1999: 16). In prison, such a 'future orientation' and 'compulsive hyperactivity' is difficult for men to achieve, and not supported by the institution. In actuality, men in prison tend to be subjected to more cyclical (and thus feminine) forms of time. Whereas femininity is linked to relational time, 'the hyperactivity of masculinity involves a transgression of the present which is swept aside in the frenetic pursuit of new challenges' (Odih 1999: 18). Yet in prison, there can be no transgression of the present—the *now* is interminably visible and confronted at all times; and there is little 'newness' in prison—such 'new challenges' tend not to exist. Thus men in prison who have cyclical time enforced upon them find themselves having—through the repetition of daily events and interactions—to face up to the temporally dislocating context that they find themselves within: an emotionally hard task.

The combination of the two forms of time may have particular implications in terms of incarcerated men's genders, being asked to interpret time in ways that are different to how their gender actually 'works' with time, ultimately making the prison experience harder on an existential level. In fact, linked to men in prison being feminised through limited spatial access (see Chapter 5), prison time has a similar feminising effect, with men sharing similar experiences to women in that 'a condition and consequence of women's subordinate position in the public sphere, and their ascribed domestic responsibilities in the private sphere, is that of significantly inhibiting their power to make decisions about their own time' (Odih 1999: 11). Men's lack of control over their own time therefore has a feminising effect upon them, by situating them in the realm of the subordinate and controlled, unable to structure their own lives, and subject to the temporal whims of masculinised staff, security, and institutional signifiers imposing controlling and cyclical routines that work against masculine temporal standards. Whereas they are used to being in the powerful position of being able to structure time themselves, their position as prisoners places them at the mercy of others' power, control, and dominance of even the most internalised and integral states of self—the passing of time.

The Masculine Value of Time

As has been noted, men and women's perceptions of time have been found to be extremely different in nature (see also Wajcman 2014). In particular, masculine time has been aligned with the control of time (Odih 1999; Shirani and Henwood 2011), individualism and instrumentalism, and looking to the future (Cottle and Klineberg 1974), in particular attempting a 'disembodiment from the particularity of human experience' (Odih 1999: 15). Such linearity, Odih continues, is central and dominant in capitalist economies, demonstrating a temporal hierarchy and the links between the definition of time and power. Such a temporal hierarchy can clearly be seen within the prison setting, in that prisoners are told what to do and when to do it, and have their daily routines mapped out with precision and predictable regularity. The instrumentality of linear time that men usually put into place in their daily lives is removed from their control, and in addition, more feminine conceptions of cyclical time are forced upon them in combination. Men, being unable to conform to this linear time-form, find themselves no longer seated within power economies embodied within temporal discourses. They become disempowered through time itself, and feminised through their subordination and lack of temporal control. This may well explain the words of one convict criminologist who states:

> Prison is a place so removed from the rhythms of the social world that temporality (experienced time) is heavily distorted. A sense of 'the future', which should be an open horizon, becomes all-but-inoperative while you are in prison (Nakagawa 1993). I think it is quite common to feel that there is no *future* within a prison sentence, nothing between going-in and coming-out but the pre-established routines, the prison timetable, to drift through. (Earle 2014: 407)

That said, there was some value ascribed to time by the men I spoke to, which was dependent upon the degree of control an individual had over it. Prisoners often described time in terms of its ownership by the particular individual serving it—time tended to belong to someone or something, hence its ascribed value:

Sebastian: But I don't want to be frank and opening up and showing my emotions to someone that is wrong in my eyes [...] Coz...someone like that don't deserve my time

Generic aspects of the prison such as the routines established and enforced, the progression of individuals through a sentence, and the development and changes to, and experienced by, individuals over time, tended to be subject to value ascription when a prisoner claimed these time signifiers as their own, or relevant to their own time experiences:

Joshua: Yeah, you know...it'll be even better once, once I get on my education the days, the days, you know, once you get your days go, everything's a...I put, I put everything into sections, you know...even my sentence, you know, do my exams, get that done, get to D Cat,[2] that...that's my goals, when you make short goals for yourself, tends to go a lot quicker I think

The achievement of such goals can be used as indicators of a positive masculine identity, as well as indicating manners in which men take control of their prison lives when such autonomy-resources are decidedly limited. The positive implications for prisoners' well-being of having a routine (and thus having time marked out formally and regularly) were also recognised with reference to the constructive use of time (in terms of using it up or gaining some form of tangible benefit, such as entering different surroundings through employment or earning money for acquiring possessions or contacting family members), although in some cases a break from the routine of prison life was also seen positively. This theme tended to be the value that participants ascribed to talking to me in the interview setting, it being something 'different' to do with one's time (and the movement into different spaces which were restricted to them—see Chapter 5).

---

[2] A lower-security prison compared to the one they were currently in.

The use and passing of time was achieved in numerous ways, most of which involved a prisoner being out of his cell (a time that was recognised as being of value) and engaged in religion, sport/gym, education, work, and so on. Achieving 'extra time' to undertake these activities was often viewed in a positive light—one prisoner spoke positively of the delay in roll call (which unfortunately shortened our interview considerably on this occasion), as it allowed him to have extra time in the gym, and the prison institution uses such views to enhance behaviour through the IEP[3] scheme. Some prisoners related the positive use of their time as being directly related to personal well-being—where a prisoner saw time in his cell as being positive, this was generally related to the concept of owner-ship of time, whereby the prisoner retained some element of control over his experiences as a result of being in his own personal space, which was also inherently linked to his masculine identity (see Chapter 5):

Researcher: So when's your favourite time of the day?
Kai: Bang up, at night
Researcher: What when the door's shut?
Kai: Yeah, bang up at night
Researcher: Why?
Kai: Coz it's your time, you know when that door's locked at eight o'clock
               that's you now till morning

Relaxation in general was seen as a positive use of time distinct to the prison sphere, and was linked by a number of participants to the prison/outside divide regarding how they saw themselves and performed their identities through the use of their time:

Sebastian: If you could come to prison for a month and then get out, that would
               be great coz you could like gather your thoughts and think right, this
               is what I'm going to do, this, that and the other because I'm like
               um…I'm classed as a prolific offender out there every day so my sort
               of licence is quite uh intensive so I have to go every day and all that
               and last time I was out they weren't really doing nothing for me it was
               sort of like a number-crunching exercise

---

[3] Incentives and Earned Privileges

Time was also viewed in a positive light when it involved personal development and self-improvement, such as time built up free from drugs, or free from disciplinary action, highlighting the positive uses of prison time and their potential to encourage future positive masculine identities with implications for how they were viewed by key audiences such as loved ones. The idea of prisoners' ages and relativity tended to be discussed by numerous individuals, generally with greater ages of others being seen to correspond to experience and maturity (and in some ways, respect), whereas younger offenders were criticised for lacking these elements. The differences between adult jail and young offenders' institutions were often described in terms of the relative increase in maturity across the estate, which in turn often resulted in a decrease in violence and the perceived need to 'prove' oneself experienced by young men (usually situated towards the bottom of a highly volatile and fragile hierarchy of masculinity). The audience available within the YOI has particularly violent and sensitive expectations of masculinity—within the adult estate, the priorities of the watching audience have altered with age (and generally with the fact that the audience watching is not invested in that individual's performances in the same way as they are within the youth estate, where young men feed off the activities and behaviours of other young men (see also Jackson 2002):

Jayden: Young offenders, yeah, um, young offenders is people feel like they've got something to prove like d'you know what I mean, I'm all this, rarara, but in a man's jail people just want to do their time [...] Get out and see their kids etc., in young offenders they all...they all think they're 50 Cent

Individuals did see their own growth in age in a negative light with reference to their ageing bodies (see Wahidin 2002; Wahidin and Tate 2005) and the impact it might have on their future identities as independent and healthy men, and who they could be to potential future audiences such as families (see also Chapter 3).

Positive, valued time in prison, therefore, tends to be time that is passed quickly or efficiently, or time that is dedicated to the individual's masculine development and thus controlled and owned by them directly and individually with positive implications for how they are *seen*. In the majority of cases, positive time seems to be related to looking forward in the life of the individual towards their aspirational future identities as free men and away from the autonomy-restricting prison context (albeit not in terms of their ageing bodies and minds):

Henry: But for me, because I have got a release date and I know that whatever happens at some point I'm getting out, it's a bit easier, but for certain people, especially on this wing, they're all lifers, people ent got release dates, they haven't got a date when they're getting out, do you know what I mean, so if, if I was in that situation I probably wouldn't like it so much, but when I know whatever happens they've got to let me out next year

Narratives that fell within the negative time theme often tended to be related to the incongruence of individuals' outside (linear) and prison (cyclical) identities, with claims that prison 'wasted' time or caused periods of stagnation:

Benjamin: It's just, it's not, it's very boring, it's very dull prison, I don't know how many people you've spoken to but it's very dull, just a waste of life

Nathan: Well I'm stuck in here I guess. I look back and I think of all the years I've wasted, I'm [X] now, I first come to prison when I'm 15 and I think that half me life, I think how much I've missed out on. At least […] I'm still young enough in a sense to go and have a life

Time tended to be regarded in a negative fashion for prisoners when it was going unused, or was not being used in a way that prisoners saw to have positive implications in relation to their future masculine identities. The costs of prison in the context of the value of their personal lives and existences were recognised, with the most negative interpretations of prison tending to be where a prisoner juxtaposed his life inside with the life he imagined himself having outside, and seeing things lacking or lost—in particular, time that was exclusively in the ownership of the prison or prison staff and out of individual control (such as time waiting for reports to be completed, routine time, or time when a prisoner was behind his door) was seen in a negative light, and prisoners often compared the negativity of their own sentences with regard to other prisoners (particularly those with a longer/less determinate situation). In addition, the negativity of time tends to change during the period of a prisoner's sentence, depending on factors both inside the prison (in terms of passing the time through achievements and development) and outside (things that prisoners are looking forward to getting out for—generally, their valued audience(s) and markers of masculinity):

Harrison: But these days because it's like the downhill part of the sentence, it just seems like it's longer, the days seem longer, the weeks are longer…at the start of my sentence they were flying by and now, coz I know now I'm so close to being back with my family, that's it […] It's starting to drag now

Another means through which men could display their masculinities was through displaying their working identities.

Working Time: Working Men

Tolson posits the male working identity as being a form of entry into a sphere of maleness:

For every man, the outcome of his socialization is his entry into work. His first day at work signifies his 'initiation' into the secretive, conspiratorial solidarity of working men. Through working, a boy, supposedly, 'becomes a man': he earns money, power, and personal independence from his family. (1977: 47)

Willis also comments on the interaction of work and masculinities, particularly manual labour, which is seen to be more masculine in comparison to 'mental work':

Manual labour is suffused with masculine qualities and given certain sensual overtones for 'the lads'. The toughness and awkwardness of physical work and effort – for itself and in the division of labour and for its strictly capitalist logic quite without intrinsic heroism or grandeur – takes on masculine lights and depths and assumes a significance beyond itself. Whatever the specific problems, so to speak, of the difficult task they are always essentially masculine problems. It takes masculine capacities to deal with them. (1977: 150)

Within the prison setting, men were given the opportunity to use their time to work. During the period of research, I observed men gardening, cleaning (a lot), serving food, picking litter, disposing of waste, and painting: in this last case, painters were obvious because they 'wore' the evidence of their trade on their clothes and bodies. In addition, there were opportunities to work in kitchens, the packing shop, motorcycle maintenance, the laundry, and so on. Men also did voluntary work at times, particularly when it came to helping others who were in need, such as on the toe-to-toe scheme to help prisoners to learn to read. Many opportunities for work were situated within what outside prison would be viewed as the domestic realm, and men's inside working identities arguably fell within what would usually be the feminine sphere, thereby placing men in a fragile gendered balance of female work being situated against masculine 'worker' identities (see Sloan 2012a, b and 2015 for more discussion on this).

Clemmer (1958) notes that there are various motives for undertaking employment within prison—profit, its social functions, prestige, and physical and mental health. In this research, work was seen as a source of money, a way to use time and get out of the cell, a way to stay active, a form of relaxation, and a way to build a routine and take control of time—all of which point towards its importance in the masculine performance and men's working towards advancing their status for particular audiences. The problems of transition in employment between the prison and the outside world, however, were noted:

Noah: ...so the way I look at it, the further you come, you know, the nearer you come, the more I should be like, you know...be working [...]in that sort of outside environment, you know. That's like, you go to work between eight and nine [...] whereas here we go to work between nine and half past, you know, and then you finish at half past eleven, you know, have your hour and a half, two hours sometimes for your lunch, and then you have two hours at work in the afternoon. And that's, you know, to me that's supposed to be preparing me for work outside

Work, therefore, clearly played a major role in the way that many participants used their time and framed their identities as men in and out of the prison, in terms of who they had been, who they currently were, and who they could be, aspired to become, or felt they were inevitably going to be (see also Sloan forthcoming).

Past, Present, and Future Men

When one considers time and masculinity more broadly, it is valuable to revisit the notion of masculinity as a fluid social construct that was discussed in Chapter 1, and to acknowledge the fact that views on what is 'masculine' have changed substantially over the years. As Kimmel notes:

> Masculinity is a constantly changing collection of meanings that we construct through our relationships with ourselves, each other, and with our world. Manhood is neither static nor timeless; it is historical. Manhood does not bubble up to consciousness from our biological makeup; it is created in culture. Manhood means different things at different times to different people. (1994: 120)

With this in mind, masculinity takes on another problematic aspect when applied to men in prison, particularly those who have been incarcerated for long periods of time—the goalposts keep changing. The expectations placed upon men and their behaviours alter regularly—new men signify the hegemonic, new fashions emerge and change their meanings,[4] and acceptable behaviours one day become the obscene or reviled the next.[5] Moral panics change the world in a second, and what was 'masculine' at the point of incarceration may not be what is expected of an individual upon their release. What sorts of men should they be becoming or aspiring to be?

The pasts, presents, and proposed futures of men are inherently connected, which poses challenges. For example, the connections between the care system and people in prison have been documented—the Social Exclusion Unit report into reducing reoffending noted that, compared to 2 % of the general population, 27 % of prisoners had been taken into care as a child (Social Exclusion Unit 2002: 18). Although not mentioned

---

[4] David Beckham wearing a sarong masculinised the item to a degree; Johnny Depp wearing eyeliner has turned make-up more manly; and skinny jeans are now worn by the most masculine of rock stars.

[5] Operation Yewtree's investigation and condemnation of former TV stars' abuse of young people, which was normalised and even 'accepted' in the 1970s, is testament to this, as is the enormous change in perceptions of what behaviours are unacceptable and racist, sexist, or homophobic.

by every participant, the importance of having experienced the care system in terms of a participant's well-being and life course was expressed on numerous occasions, in terms of the influence that it had upon the individual's family connections (both past and future generations) and personal identity. The impact that a lack of parental stability or role models had upon a number of men was clearly substantial, with implications for aspects of their masculine identity such as their abilities as fathers or sons—it clearly mattered when they had not been the audience of importance to the men who were significant in their own lives as they grew up (see also Phillips 2012: 163).

Other participants recognised the unique skills that their experiences of care provided them:

Jude: [...] sometimes you've got to have been there to know how to deal with things...the best, best member of staff that I met in the children's home was someone I met who had been in care, who had been in prison himself and, and knew, you know you've got to be there sometimes

Isaac: It's just a way of life ent it, coz when I, coz from a young age I was brought up in care and things like that, in secure units, detention centres and everything like that, so I just learnt to live by myself, by my own rules, and I've learnt to live on the street as well, you know what I mean, you pick things up on the street, so I'm very streetwise, me, you know what I mean, so that's just how it is

The accounts participants gave of their experiences of care were generally negative, although some tried to interpret them positively. Despite this, the influences of being within the care system away from their homes, parental role models, or guidance, and the lack of 'normal' legitimate masculinity development, clearly link to criminality and their current positions in prison:

Zachary: And like there's a connection between that, like social services, such as like going into care from your, from your like your own home, and then um peer pressure kind of brings drugs into the circle, and then you just find yourself in a little vicious circle

When it came to talking about the crimes they had committed and their pathways into prison, many spoke of how drink and drugs in particular had played a major part in their offending behaviour, causing them to commit crimes to support their habits or as a result of being intoxicated and lacking full awareness and responsibility. Appleton found similar problematic starts to her participants' lives, what she termed 'contaminated beginnings' (2010: 143). It has been claimed that:

> a close relationship exists between delinquency/criminality, specific life-style and heavy drinking. These three factors seem to interact and to enhance each other in the sense of an increasing spiral, which leads to a decrease in opportunities for developing and maintaining a normal, socially integrated biography. (Kerner et al. 1997: 416)

These two factors (drink and drugs) seemed to play the greatest role in individuals' accounts of their offending pasts:

Isaac: […] I was doing a lot of cocaine as well, ecstasy…crack cocaine now and then, you know it was just getting out of hand, really out of hand…a lot of drink as well, I was doing a lot of drink, d'you know what I mean it was just, like the lifestyle […]

It is clear that there was a cyclical aspect to some criminal lives and a degree of chaos featured in the past lives of many offenders—intriguing when considering the idea that cyclical time is actually 'feminine time' (Maines and Hardesty 1987). Some spoke directly about the part that family (through arguments, retaliation, role model behaviour, abuse, and the protection of relationships) played in the shaping of their current identities, and friendships and peers too played a key role, with some blaming their offending upon the influences of others. Regarding the influence of others upon identity development, many participants positioned their offending in terms of difference from other prisoners, using concepts such as being in the 'wrong place and the wrong time', offences being a 'one off', a 'mistake', a result of 'bad choices' or circumstances, compared to persistent offenders. Although many did see their offending actions as having been serious enough to merit a prison sentence (albeit not always of the length given), many did see themselves as different from the 'normal' male prisoner:

Harvey: me I'm not, I'm, I'm in prison but I'm not a criminal criminal like […] People out robbing, thieving and, I've never ever gone out robbing…to get money or nothing like that, the only crime I've committed is violence, which is pub fights

So violence and fighting are seen as acceptable male behaviours, not wholly 'criminal', whilst other crimes (often committed by 'others') were unacceptable. Some participants did refer to their offences and imprisonment in terms of not being proud of them, and feeling like they had changed (or had to change) with age. Such notions of pride, differentiation, and distancing are processes occurring for others: they are performances, or the outcomes of performances, directed at certain audiences whose values and opinions about them they value.

Many participants had already served time in prison on numerous occasions and many found a form of justification for their offending pasts, such as drink, drugs, the influences of others, criminal justice procedures, or their age and immaturity. A few spoke of the fact that they had learned that they struggled to manage negative emotions effectively (with some speaking of how therapy and courses had allowed them to address their offending behaviour patterns and their pathways into crime, and had helped them to learn to address such feelings). In fact, this explanation of criminality fits well with the fact that many participants had clearly gone through problematic life experiences in the past, and had little stability or opportunities for legitimately gaining masculine identities:

Samuel: It was an escalation, escalation of my past offending when I was a child, a teenager, and then I had a period for about 12 years where I kind of managed to settle down, get myself a job, married…just basically living a normal life, but…just under the surface there was issues that I didn't deal with as a kid, and…the feeling of frustration, and guilt within my marriage, and the inability to deal with negative emotions, um…just came out one night when I'd had too much to drink […]

Thus, masculinity played a key role in their past life course, positive efforts at domesticity and negative responses to emotions, and their incarcerated sense of self, influencing which aspects of their offending pasts they were willing to confront, how, and why.

In addition to this, many men showed obvious anxiety related to their future masculine lives, which were directly linked to past masculinities—their own, in terms of how criminal convictions would impact upon their future lives, but also others' masculinities. Some spoke of the past masculinities of gang members or rival criminals—people who used to be audiences that mattered to them—and the impact these individuals could have on their ability to establish a legitimate, settled, non-criminal masculinity upon their release (at least in the same place that they lived before). Others spoke of their fathers in terms of negative masculinities—and their lack of positive role models for how they should 'be' men—or positive masculinities—in terms of being 'good' men who they felt they had 'let down'.

As such, somewhat contrary to the remarks noted by Earle (2014) at the start of this chapter, the men did look to the future. This may be a result of the type of prison that I was in—a category C training prison is, by its nature, attempting to 'train' individuals for their future lives out of prison, and there were numerous courses and opportunities to work and learn that looked ahead to when these men would be released. That said, it is not always a given that training prisons provide sufficient or suitable opportunities for improved lives. Participants' futures played an influential role in the framing of their narratives about their experiences of prison, being something that they could use their time in prison to add value to through work, reflection and personal development. In particular, many participants spoke of their aspirations and plans for the future and their future success, often tied in to their career hopes and, essentially, who they wanted to become with reference to the management of working identities and the creation of the potential for legitimate masculinity markers (such as the ability to have a working identity, earn money, provide for the family, and accrue wealth):

Zachary: […] that's the career, my end objective if you like is probably to like open a gym […] If I could do that then…that would be me, that would be all my dreams come true

Participants' aspirational identities were often linked to the prison experiences and the opportunities available to them for the use of their time. Some voiced concerns about the validity of the training that they received in prison and its usefulness on the outside, highlighting the potential limits to the value of their used time. Numerous participants discussed their anxieties with regard to attaining work upon release, and the importance of having options and something to fall back on, and so the avoidance of a future criminal (and prisoner) identity and the creation of a legitimate means of being masculine. Other anxieties for the future included finding housing directly after release (with extended implications for their identities as independent and self-sufficient men), and the concept of release in general provoked anxiety in a number of participants, particularly those who had spent a long time in prison, and those who saw themselves as institutionalised (lacking the ability to express individuality, control over the self, or the skills to be a legitimate male) in one way or another:

George: I'm a clean man, I have a clean heart, I show emotions…I don't know man, I see, I don't know, I don't know how I would feel if I go out there I'm scared, I'm, I'm…I'm shitting my load man when every day I think about it, one day they're going to let me out, what am I going to be like man? And like she's telling me look you're going to be alright, everyone's […] and I'm like nah man, I'm going to be scared for the rest of my…I don't know man, thinking about it now my heart's staring to shake and that, that's how badly I'm scared man, coz I know that it's coming close now…I've been away for a long time. […] I hated it out there man. I didn't feel safe but I did do what I liked, I did do good out there

The future of prisoners in terms of their being reunited with their families was a major emergent theme in interviews—the importance of the family as a legitimate masculine identity signifier and in terms of coping in prison and having something to work towards was evident, particularly with reference to children (who, in part, played a role as signifiers of their fathers' masculine virility, or a potential key audience for their identities). Friendships on the outside were not seen in the same light—a number of prisoners spoke of putting their current friendships on hold as a form of test, or ending them completely, often sacrificing seeing them so that they could see their families instead, due to the limited nature of visiting orders.[6] They controlled their social spheres and managed the available identity signifiers as a form of gendered currency[7]—families have the potential to say more about male identities than friends:

Harrison: Rang all my mates and was just like, look, I can't deal with any of you coming up, just…anyway, that's a better way coz I'll see who my true friends are when I get out and see if they're still around, d'you know what I mean?

Prisoners have to overcome the difficulties that occur with respect to maintaining their aspirational identity performances, formed in the prison through reflection and personal development that occur through the use of prison time, when outside and subjected to other identity-shaping events and activities. Many prisoners made plans for the future, both tangible and intangible, and although such plans for eventual resettlement and the future were significant to many, some prisoners did view their outside futures with a degree of scepticism, emphasising the difficulties in masculine identity transmission across the prison divide:

Kevin: […] prison's at the back of your mind, it's not something that you're not going, it ain't to say that you're not going to get going now and again, but it's at the back of your mind, you don't think that there's fences going round and you're going behind bars and you're going to be locked up and have to go about this and have to queue for your food, you could be degraded and, and wearing what you're supposed to and doing what you're supposed to do, and uh it's just that's one of the main things in prison, you actually forget when you're released when, in the outside world and you're like…all this going on and you've got responsibilities and you've got that and you, you, you're so engrossed in what you're doing…

Jayden: In a way I don't, I don't ever want to come back but now I've got a criminal record it's harder to get jobs and that out there, so […] …dunno really. If you can't get a job and…it's hard, d'you know what I mean… […] …everyone needs money to survive, so…dunno what's round the corner do ya

---

[6] Prisoners are only allowed a certain number of visitors per month, which are organised through the use of visiting orders, sent out to prospective visitors.
[7] Many thanks to Ben Raikes for his insights on this issue.

The majority of concerns with the future that were discussed in interviews regarded prisoners' wishes to return to a sense of normality, highlighting the severe abnormality of the prison as experienced by many. Some prisoners spoke of looking forward to activities that would be classed as normal by the majority of us: shopping, seeing new films in the cinema, going to watch football teams and undertaking sports, buying cars, going to church, expanding the family, and enjoying non-prison food and cutlery (all of which are markers of masculine hegemony with respect to the acquisition of wealth signifiers, virility, physicality, independent living, etc.). Yet it is important to recognise that the pace of life changes over the course of a man's incarceration—those electronic gadgets that men aspire to own that signify wealth and masculine prowess through engagement with digital capitalism can actually increase the pace of life (Wajcman 2014). The longer a man is in prison, the harder it may be to adapt to the change in pace upon release that engagement with digital elements requires, thereby alienating men further from processes of integration, normalisation, and the assertion of capitalist priorities:

Gabriel: […] all new to us ent it, when I came in you know what I mean…12 years ago and where I come from […] we didn't have coffee shops and all these Subways and everything, we had McDonald's and everything but that would have only just been coming in all these coffee shops and everything […] They just weren't around

Researcher: So Starbucks and things like that

Gabriel: Yeah they were just starting up you know what I mean, you had them in London but they ain't got out to the certain world where I live and everything so you didn't, you didn't have it…know what I mean so it's all new to me. Oh phones, bloody hell when I came in phones were that size and you know what I mean, there weren't cameras and internet on them and all this sort of thing, baffles me, I'm lost, have trouble just dialling the number on the damn thing, that's about the only thing I can do with them, so technology's all changed you know what I mean […] Flat-screen TVs and all this sort of thing, stuck on the wall nah, weren't about when…I came to prison. So all that's is like changed you know what I mean

Reflexive Note

Being in prison also impacted upon *me* in relation to time experiences. In terms of my observations of time in the prison setting, I sometimes found myself losing track of time due to the lack of markers available to me, and I started to regulate my days in the prison according to the segments of time divided up by prison 'movements'. Although the prison day was strictly divided up into sections of time defined according to these 'movements', such sections were not always uniform in character, being dictated by matters of security. Roll check after a movement—the counting up of prisoners after everyone has moved to their next location of the day—was often late, which would shorten the following segment of time. As Medlicott observed, means of marking time through the routine of the prison day are not necessarily consistent, with potential negative effects:

> So the time-markers are trivial matters, such as the television going on. Even these markers are tenuous and unreliable, since they lie within the control of the staff, a power which they exercise as a weapon in the maintenance of conformity. (1999: 227)

Although such time markers were useful in terms of knowing the structure of the day, they also acted both as restrictions and a means through which to situate people within the prison institution through the imposition of controlling time regimes, including myself as a researcher. Restrictions in that they took away freedom to move away from the set structure of the day—if it was time for movement, you moved, even if there was scope to continue working on whatever was occupying you at the time, such as a research interview. I had no control over this, and was essentially under the highly masculinised control of prison security forces—quite a disempowering sensation. Numerous interviews had to be cut short as a result of having to stick to the set time frame as a result of the needs of security—security was thus inherently connected to time, in that the population of the prison was regulated according to roll calls at set times during the day.

Time markers acted as a monotonous controlling agent with serious security implications if they were not conformed to—controlling prisoners, staff, and visitors alike. As a researcher, the research agenda was out of my control to some degree—interviews had to be set within the set periods of time dictated by the prison security remit. In addition, the time markers had implications for me as an individual, acting as a rapid acclimatiser to the institutional regime and setting my internal clock to that of the prison in a relatively quick period of time. I became part of the prison through conforming to its regime and working to its timetable without really thinking about it.

Strangely, I had not thought about the impact of prison time upon me in a gendered fashion until I left the prison and began writing this book, other than in terms of the practicalities. When one considers the imposition of combination time patterns (i.e. cyclical *and* linear) upon individuals, this does explain some of the tensions I experienced whilst in the prison that I could not articulate at the time. There was something constricting—both practically and on a more existential level—about the routines even for those who could walk away, and rarely did those routines feel like they considered the people as opposed to the institutional requirements: there was something inhuman about the way that time was divided into equal segments. Hall makes the point that, as a result of us transferring our conceptions of time in modern day from our body clocks to timepieces, and then to have considered those clocks on the wall to be the 'reality', we have created stresses and conflicts within ourselves:

> We have now constructed an entire complex system of schedules, manners, and expectations to which we are trying to adjust ourselves, when, in reality, it should be the other way around. The culprit is extension transference. Because of extension transference, the schedule is the reality and people and their needs are not considered (Hall 1983: 131).

Nowhere is this more true than in the modern-day prison.

For me as a woman, I am more attuned to working on cyclical time, which arguably also directed my approach to research and interviewing—the ethnographic process is arguably both cyclical and linear, looking forward but also immersing the researcher within controlling regimes.[8] Adapting to linearity and the hyperregulation of cyclicality was an additional challenge that

---

[8] Many thanks to Jamie Irving for helping me with this thought process.

is hardly ever discussed in the research methods literature. Time and its gendered impacts is clearly something that ought to be given some consideration beyond simply fatigue and practicality when undertaking prisons research.

Summary

This chapter brings the notion of masculinity to considerations of time in a manner that is lacking in academic discourse—the gendered implications of time as punishment for men are severe and distinct in terms of the impact upon masculine identity signifiers and the resultant implications. Whilst consideration has obviously been given to the negative ramifications for male identities—these being at the very heart of the nature and purpose of incarceration—consideration has also been given to the positive implications of prison time, such as personal development opportunities, which often go unrecognised within academic discussion. Men saw time often in terms of who they were or who they could become as men—'potential masculinities'—and the control and ownership of time was crucial in processes of differentiation from the prisoner identity and the negotiation and application of masculine signifiers of work, fatherhood, (hetero)sexual relationships, and independent living to both their past, present, and future lives.

Time is highly significant in the prison experience and masculine identity management, whether that be in terms of prisoners' aspirations for the future use of their time, their return to a sense of the norm and their personal development, or how the prisoner interprets his time in the context of his ageing body, sense of autonomy, or expectations of self (relative to his actual position, or the positions of others both in and out of prison). The ownership and control of such time by prisoners is, therefore, extremely influential upon interpretations of the prison experience, as prisoners will evaluate their prison careers according to the positivity and negativity of time they endure, and the length of time they have to suffer or enjoy such time markers (and the values of marking time at all).

Where time is not owned or controlled, individuals are made very aware of the reduced control they have over their own masculine potential in terms of self-improvement and development in readiness for their future non-prison lives and identities. The prison experience, by its very nature, attempts to reduce the individuality of an offender by subsuming them into the prison community, where the rules, routines, and surroundings are generically enforced upon all prisoners; however, the experience itself is also individual, according to the values prisoners place upon their time in and out of the prison. The gendered experience of time and its conflicts has huge implications for this process of experience. I have tried to demonstrate this in this chapter by considering both the wider-scale notions of time and its imposition upon the prison, as well as more individualised understandings emanating from men's testimonies.

Time, therefore, can have major implications: the ways in which an individual spends their time can impact upon the value of that time, and in turn, the value of such time spent in prison can impact upon the ways in which prisoners choose to spend their time—making use of it, being violent, or claiming ownership of it.

References

Appleton, C. (2010). *Life after life imprisonment.* Oxford University Press: Oxford.

Clemmer, D. (1958). *The prison community* (Newth ed.). New York: Holt, Reinhart and Winston.

Cohen, S., & Taylor, L. (1972). *Psychological survival: The experience of long-term imprisonment.* Middlesex, Maryland and Victoria: Penguin Books Ltd.

Cottle, T. J. (1976). *Perceiving time: A psychological investigation with men and women.* New York, London, Sydney and Toronto: John Wiley & Sons.

Cottle, T. J., & Klineberg, S. L. (1974). *The present of things future: Explorations of time in human experience.* New York: The Free Press.

Daly, K. J. (1996). *Families and time: Keeping pace in a hurried culture.* Thousand Oaks, CA: SAGE Publications.

Earle, R. (2014). Insider and out: Making sense of a prison experience and a research experience. *Qualitative Inquiry, 20*(4), 404–413.

Giddens, A. (1981). *A contemporary critique of historical materialism: Vol. 1: Power, property and the state.* London and Basingstoke: The Macmillan Press Ltd.

Hall, E. T. (1983). *The dance of life: The other dimension of time.* New York: Doubleday.

HM Inspectorate of Prisons. (2012). *Expectations: Criteria for assessing the treatment of prisoners and conditions in prisons.* Retrieved January, 2014 from http://www.justice.gov.uk/downloads/about/hmipris/adult-expectations-2012.pdf

Inciardi, J. A., Martin, S. S., Butzin, C. A., Hooper, R. M., & Harrison, L. D. (1997). An effective model of prison-based treatment for drug-involved offenders. *Journal of Drug Issues, 27*(2), 261–278.

Jackson, C. (2002). 'Laddishness' as a self-worth protection strategy. *Gender and Education, 14*(1), 37–50.

Kerner, H.-J., Weitekamp, E. G. M., Stelly, W., & Thomas, J. (1997). Patterns of criminality and alcohol abuse: results of the Tuebingen Criminal Behaviour Development Study. *Criminal Behaviour and Mental Health, 7,* 401–420.

Kimmel, M. S. (1994). Masculinity as homophobia: Fear, shame, and silence in the construction of gender identity. In H. Brod & M. Kaufman (Eds.), *Theorizing masculinities.* Thousand Oaks and London: Sage.

Maines, D. R., & Hardesty, M. J. (1987). Temporality and gender: Young adults' career and family plans. *Social Forces, 66*(1), 102–120.

Matthews, R. (2009). *Doing time: An introduction to the sociology of imprisonment* (2nd ed.). Basingstoke and New York: Palgrave Macmillan.

Medlicott, D. (1999). Surviving in the time machine: Suicidal prisoners and the pains of prison time. *Time and Society, 8*(2), 211–230.

Medlicott, D. (2008). Time. In Y. Jewkes & J. Bennett (Eds.), *Dictionary of prisons and punishment.* Cullompton: Willan Publishing.

Ministry of Justice. (2013). *Story of the prison population 1993-2012 England and Wales*, Ministry of Justice Statistics Bulletin, Ministry of Justice. Retrieved November, 2015 from https://www.gov.uk/government/publications/story-of-the-prison-population-1993-2012

Moran, D. (2012). Prisoner reintegration and the stigma of prison time inscribed on the body. *Punishment and Society, 14*(5), 564–583.

Nakagawa, G. (1993). Deformed subjects, docile bodies: Disciplinary practices and subject-constitution in stories of Japanese American internment. In D. K. Mumby (Ed.), *Narrative and social control: Critical perspectives.* London, England: Sage.

Odih, P. (1999). Gendered time in the age of deconstruction. *Time and Society, 8*(1), 9–38.

Phillips, C. (2012). *The multicultural prison: Ethnicity, masculinity and social relations among prisoners.* Oxford: Oxford University Press.

Schmid, T. J., & Jones, R. S. (1991). Suspended Identity: Identity transformation in a maximum security prison. *Symbolic Interaction, 14*(4), 415–432.

Shirani, F., & Henwood, K. (2011). Taking one day at a time: Temporal experiences in the context of unexpected life course transitions. *Time and Society,* *20*(1), 49–68.

Sloan, J. (2012a). 'You Can See Your Face in My Floor': Examining the function of cleanliness in an adult male prison. *The Howard Journal of Criminal Justice,* *51*(4), 400–410.

Sloan, J. (2012b). Cleanliness, spaces and masculine identity in an adult male prison. *Prison Service Journal, 201,* 3–6.

Sloan, J. (2015). Masculinity, imprisonment and working identities. In C. Reeves (Ed.), *Experiencing imprisonment: Research on the experience of living and working in carceral institution.* London and New York: Routledge.

Sloan, J. (Forthcoming). Aspirational masculinities. In Robinson, A. & Hamilton, P. (Eds.), *Transforming identities.*

Social Exclusion Unit. (2002). *Reducing re-offending by ex-prisoners.* London: Social Exclusion Unit.

The Prison Rules. (1999). Statutory Instrument 1999 No. 728.

Tolson, A. (1977). *The limits of masculinity.* London: Tavistock Publications Limited.

Wahidin, A. (2002). Reconfiguring older bodies in the prison time machine. *Journal of Aging and Identity,* *7*(3), 177–193.

Wahidin, A. (2006). Time and the prison experience. *Sociological Research Online,* *11*(1). Retrieved November, 2015 from http://www.socresonline.org.uk/11/1/wahidin.html

Wahidin, A., & Tate, S. (2005). Prison (E)scapes and body tropes: Older women in the prison time machine. *Body and Society, 11*(2), 59–79.

Wajcman, J. (2014). *Pressed for time: The acceleration of life in digital capitalism.* Chicago and London: University of Chicago Press.

Willis, P. (1977). *Learning to labour: How working class kids get working class jobs.* Farnborough: Saxon House, Teakfield Limited.

Wilson, A. (2010). Interrupted life: The criminal justice system as a disruptive force on the lives of young offenders. *Prison Service Journal, 189,* 3–8.

5

Spatial Masculinities

Spaces have a fundamental impact upon the prison experience. Many carceral geographers have considered the ways in which spaces are constructed and defined within the prison sphere, from being central to power relations (Sibley and van Hoven 2009), to the importance of vision and relations with others (van Hoven and Sibley 2008), or even as being indistinct with the outside, with incarceration being 'a dynamic and often contradictory state of betweenness' (Baer and Ravneberg 2008: 205). What is rarely considered is how these spaces and their use is, ultimately, highly gendered. Prisons in England are, in the majority, spaces designed for adult men (and adult men in the 1800s in a number of cases), and so can be extremely unsuitable for women and young offenders (Corston 2007). They are hardly perfect for adult men in the twenty-first century either.

In addition to their often outdated and security-focused design, what prisons tend to result in for adult men is the imposition of feminine spatial control. In general men and women have different accessibility to different public and private spaces: in the majority of cases, men have access and women are restricted. For example, women are not meant to walk alone on the street at night, whereas men are never challenged for such behaviours; women are expected to remain in 'safe' domestic spaces,

© The Editor(s) (if applicable) and The Author(s) 2016
J.A. Sloan, *Masculinities and the Adult Male Prison Experience*,
DOI 10.1057/978-1-137-39915-1_5

whereas 'boys will be boys', and men are much less problematised for their location outside the domestic setting, etc.) Yet, in spite of the recognition that the public and private are inherently gendered dimensions, and that this becomes problematised when contextualised in the prison, which is both public and private in nature (Janssen 2005), the masculinity and male use of such male spaces and the impact of that tends to go unnoticed. Even the use of non-spaces can demonstrate masculinities—rough sleeping and homelessness can be symbolic of masculine strength and reliance through the lack of 'space' (Higate 2000).

Spatiality, Power, and Resistance

What tends to link masculinities and prison spaces is the notion of institutional power imposed upon prisoners and the subsequent resistances that are made to these impositions (Dirsuweit 1999). More often than not, such resistance is framed in the negative, rather than as a process of using the prison space for personal well-being. In reality, the prevalence of security narratives and the focus on dangerousness that pervades discussions of male prisoners has the outcome that men are prevented from seeking more positive signifiers of masculinity such as children and families (Curtis 2014). In this research, however, many participants spoke of the importance of attaining education, qualifications, training, therapy, or some other form of learning whilst in prison, in order to achieve something positive with their time and a degree of masculine self-sufficiency and legitimate identity status in terms of planning for their release (see Chapter 4). This 'learning' was not always totally positive in terms of being socially legitimate behaviours, yet could be considered positive with respect to the development of masculine independence and self-defence as personal safety mechanisms—some spoke of learning to assert themselves and their identity through violence:

Henry: You can learn things from being in prison, you can…like obviously probably not the good things to learn but…you can get a bit street smart in prison, you can get…you, you can learn to look after yourself and like not be intimidated by people and standing up for yourself, I mean because the size that I am, like

I'm quite a small fella, ah, growing up and in young offenders institutes as well I used to get like into a lot of situations where…I'd come off second best, but as I've done so many years in prison…the more recent things and confrontations I'm involved in, I'm…more the aggressor now than in the past I'm on the receiving end of it [...] Because I've just learnt to sort of toughen up and just how to react to people and how to speak to people if you feel they're taking the piss or whatever, how, how a, how to put it on people and how to fight as well, d'you know what I mean, like the more fights you have, the more you get the hang of it, and the more you get the hang of it, the better you get, d'you know what I mean?

A number of participants noted the negative aspects of incarceration in spatial terms, describing it as being highly stressful, frustrating, and like a trap (e.g. a lack of autonomy and independence, as noted by Sykes [1958]):

Zachary: You know, just sit in your cell it's just lonely and you can't help but think and you don't really want to think coz thinking just drives you mad, but it's just…it's the worst punishment going is to be in the seg,[1] you know, it just drives you mad

The prison is unique in terms of its spatial make-up and operation—rarely, even in other institutions, are people forced to occupy certain spaces as punishment, where these spaces have been designed not for well-being, health, or enjoyment, but for security and punishment (see Shalev 2013 for the extreme manipulation of spaces in supermax prisons in the USA). Although other countries try to change penal environments to focus less on these considerations and more upon rehabilitation (Jewkes and Moran 2014), in England we still focus primarily on the security aspect.

Spatial Security: Spatial Limits

Security is paramount to the entire process of prison: the three objectives of HM Prison Service, as detailed in its statement of purpose, are:

"To protect the public and provide what commissioners want to purchase by:

---

[1] Referring to the segregation unit.

- Holding prisoners securely
- Reducing the risk of prisoners re-offending
- Providing safe and well-ordered establishments in which we treat prisoners humanely, decently and lawfully."

(HM Prison Service Statement of Purpose)

As such, the formal security of prisoners is officially acknowledged to be of fundamental importance, yet insecurity is key to the prison experience and the manner in which it is represented in the media and popular culture. Prisons are notoriously violent spaces, with such violence being observed by the majority of participants in one form or another—most were simply observers/audience, but some described their personal experiences as victims of theft, violence, or bullying, whilst others spoke of the part they played in committing violent acts towards staff and other prisoners, particularly at early points in long sentences. Many spoke of the presence of weapons, phones, drugs, and so on, which negatively influenced the security of the prisoners, in spite of the prison itself being seen by some to be more formally secure than many other category C prisons. Those who observed violence and harm to others often spoke of the way that it influenced, shocked, and changed them, wishing to avoid such a fate themselves:

Researcher: So what made you change to do that?

Bailey: Um probably when I was in [prison] my pal got stabbed up, um and he's in a, he's in a wheelchair now and he got like hundred and ninety-seven stitches in his neck, face, back, all over but they'd doubled the razor, so they doubled the razor up so they couldn't stitch it so he had months of…um, where he just had gauzes on him so they had to change them every day, plus where they'd been kicking him he couldn't walk again so he was in a wheelchair as well, so that was over, phh a stupid bit of debt, do you know what I mean…after that I just calmed down a bit

Those serving long or indeterminate sentences in particular also spoke of their need to avoid such trouble due to the potential impact it could have upon their chances of release and outside expectations. Some participants spoke of the use of violence against themselves, others, or prison property as a means of achieving some form of physical security through segregation from others, and many participants spoke of the ways in which they had changed and adapted in order to avoid such violence. The majority described changing their performed masculine personas and becoming physically and emotionally hardened in order to avoid the risk of being seen to be weak or a potential victim, and to prove or obtain a tough reputation.

Thus, individuals' performed identities, such as hardness, physical strength, violence, and dominance, became their security against others—it was more about how they made use of physical spaces than how those spaces made them secure:

William: You can't be yourself completely in here, you can't let your guard down sometimes, even with other inmates you have to, d'you know sometimes put on a bit of a different persona coz otherwise it can leave you open to attack and…yeah, that's just prison in general though

The importance of security of identity and its links to spatial dimensions was also recognised. A number of participants spoke of the distinct sense of emotional security that they felt in therapeutic environments, highlighting the hidden emotional insecurity that they had to experience in the 'normal' prison environment where they had to police their behaviours—certain prison spaces were emotionally 'safer' than others, and this will have direct implications for the success (and failure) for many offending behaviour/therapeutic programmes that require any degree of emotional engagement, particularly in front of others.

Security was clearly visible in the prison in terms of locks, gates, fences, and staff observations—on a day-to-day basis I had to pass through many doors in front of many eyes and had to ensure that I preserved my own security, the security of my property, and the security of others. As Martin recognises:

Researchers may be trained to remember detailed information for their study, but they often forget they are under as much scrutiny as their subjects. Prisons are like goldfish bowls – everything that happens is seen and talked about by a large number of other people. (2000: 225)

Security was, as to be expected, particularly noticeable when I visited the segregation unit, where prisoners were kept separate for the protection of others (rather than the protection of themselves). Prisoners had restricted access to potential weapons such as nail clippers or chairs (the image of the chair for prisoners in the interview room on the segregation unit has remained with me for a long time—it was bolted to the floor). It is clear that the maintenance of physical and emotional security is of concern to prisoners, be that by proving themselves not to be victims, or by attempting to avoid trouble, in both cases avoiding negative gender identity labels. Trouble nevertheless pervades the prison experience through personal or vicarious victimisation and violence (both in the prison and experienced on the outside), and it has far-reaching consequences for the prison experience:

Bailey: … but how you get brought up in life, if you see violence, you perpetuate violence, you use it because that's all you know

Masculinity and the Prison Cell

One place that prisoners spoke about as a place that they could potentially feel more 'safe', and where they could remove their assumed fronts (see Chapter 3) was in the cell—in this prison, generally being single occupancy and thus 'private' spaces. The prison cell is a key iconic image in the representation of punishment—it can be the 'home' of a prisoner for up to 23 hours a day; as Henderson notes, 'under any system, the cell is the essential unit of the prison' (1911: 62). During the research, I had the opportunity to see a number of cells and was surprised by the amount of personality that individuals put into them. Some men took pride in taking ownership of their space and keeping it clean and tidy. The imposition of elements of individuals' personalities upon their 'personal' space helps to overcome the lack of true ownership that individuals in prison can actually have over their cells, these being spaces that are used and reused by many others on a regular basis (see Sloan 2012a, b). There was an element of sadness about them, particularly the smaller cells, and the first time I saw a cell on the main jail has remained with me throughout my experience:

*One of my bleakest moments—I got to go on the wing today and actu-
ally saw into a cell. So small. Smell. Dark. Despair.* (Research Diary 1,
June 2009)

Participants tended to speak about their cells as an area that they
socialised and ate in, seeing it as their personal space. This ownership was
expressed through the direct influence of the individual over his cell,
through cleaning and tidying, and through the content of personal
possessions for comfort in addition to being signs of wealth (see Baer
2005 and Crewe 2009), such as soft furnishings, duvets, video game con-
soles, toiletries, and so on. The display of pictures, certificates showing
successes, and photographs of family, friends, women, and so on, were
prolific, signifying an individual's role in the family or successes in
heterosexual relationships, which were distinct to the individuals'
emotional needs and personal tastes (when it came to the display of girls
and football teams, for example). All of these also served a purpose for
any potential audience who visited the cell. In spite of this, however, the
prison still maintained overarching control of the site, as they enforced
restrictions on the positioning of pictures on notice boards, for example.
As such, the cell as personal space was rarely seen as fully owned. Sharing
meant privacy and hygiene might be sacrificed and even single occupancy
meant a lavatory in the living space. Some saw this as a reason not to
make their cells too comfortable. In addition, some felt that making one's
cell too like home meant that they were too settled in the prison environment, which they saw to be a negative indicator of institutionalisation.
Many men spoke of the fact that they painted (or wanted to paint) their
cells in order to expunge previous inhabitants' detritus:

Joshua: That's the worst thing because when you come in, the guy who had the cell
          before me, he must, he lived like a pig. The place was a pigsty, it really was a
          pigsty, I'm not joking […] So, you know, it would, just to clean it that bit
          better, if you could paint it and then it would be mine, you know?

That said, the cell as personal space was also seen to be a place of safety
and relaxation. There was some debate about whether time locked in
one's cell was positive or negative. On the one hand, individuals tended

to state that they felt safe in their cells (particularly when they had keys and could protect their possessions from 'pad thieves'), they were able to relax and show emotion, and they were able to take down the front that they felt it was necessary to put up for other prisoners:

Kai: D'you know what I mean, but…nah you can't, you can't be yourself…unless you're behind your door […] But what can you be yourself about behind your door, nowt really is it […] Apart from looking at four walls and watching a bit of telly […] You know that is the only time you can really relax and take that, and take that front down, to be honest with you

Some felt the cell was a form of retreat from the prison setting, with the policing of this space resulting in it taking on a separate character to the wider prison context:

Samuel: No…no it's it's hard, obviously being in this environment, um, because… there, there is a lot of negativity that flies around…flies round the wing, flies around the jail, um…so…I, I as soon, soon as my door's locked, on the night-time…it's like I can just lay on my bed and go (sigh)…you know, like that sigh when I first come in here… […] …it's just, like, I'm back in my own space now, and it's time to relax…because I think when you're on the wing you do have to put up a certain…although I, I put up a certain guard…I, I, I still allow myself to be who I am…and, you know, and don't let it get in the way of how I conduct myself on the wing or how people see me

The (single) cell, then, can be seen to be a space in which prisoners are able to be more of themselves, surrounded by their own possessions, and able to think their own thoughts (though these are not always positive) away from the rest of the prison. Prisoners made cells their own through the manipulation of this space, which also allowed them to maintain a sense of certainty and security in a place that they had the maximum control over, albeit still a small space that is repeatedly used by others and thus never truly singularly 'owned' by the individual. Some took control over this space in a destructive manner when they were stressed, through flooding or smashing the cell up, again highlighting the fact that this is one of the only places in the prison where a prisoner can express his true feelings and sense of self:

George: We want proper, make us feel comfortable in our cell, this is our home…
            for the next…God knows how many years, but we have to feel comfort-
            able in our own cells, we're allowed to buy rugs…electric shavers, electric
            toothbrushes, stereos, better rugs

It is also one of the only places in the prison where men can take control of their lives by giving up control in a very personal way—through sleep. Many participants spoke of the positive aspects of being asleep during their time in prison—one particularly tired-looking prisoner noted, '*That's one good thing about prison—you can sleep til you like*'. The concept of sleeping in prison has been discussed in the academic literature, although generally from the perspective of insomnia and the potential negative effects (Cope 2003; Elger 2004; Warren et al. 2004; Ireland and Culpin 2006). In the context of this research, participants spoke of the activity of sleeping in positive terms—a way in which to pass time, to recharge after a stressful day in the prison environment, and a way in which they could escape from the awareness of being in prison and the need to perform their gendered identities:

Researcher: What's your favourite time of day when you're in prison then? Weird
              question
Henry: When I'm asleep […] coz then you're not in prison are ya […] So
              obviously when you're asleep you don't, you're not in prison, you're
              asleep, ent ya, and the worst time for me is when I wake up, every
              morning I wake up it's horrible, I get like a feeling in my stomach, I
              just look round and see bars and, oh it's horrible

Sleeping was a key coping mechanism used by many participants to 'escape', and waking up (or being woken) in the morning was often referred to negatively with regard to the spaces that they awoke to find themselves within. In addition, sleeping was seen to be a way in which participants could take control of their time, describing it as their own, with many ascribing particular value to the weekends when (if they worked during the week) they could choose to sleep for as long as they liked. This was particularly evident in the narratives of long-term prisoners. Time when others were asleep was also valued in terms of the peace it brought, although some did make note of the security concerns that were present when they chose to sleep—participants referred to locking their doors, and one participant who was unable to lock his door spoke of experiencing being victimised while he slept.

Not being able to sleep as a result of their worries and concerns led to numerous participants undertaking activities in order to distract the mind (such as listening to music) or wear themselves out (such as work or the gym). Sleep was, therefore, of value to participants, in that it shaped their activities during the day, whist also providing a mechanism in which they were able to take control of their lives in some way. Unusually, this manner of taking control was achieved by the action of complete avoidance of control, as sleeping makes individuals vulnerable (and hence not masculine)—hence the security concerns expressed—and removes them from the realm of responsibility and performance—we generally do not care (or know) who is watching when we sleep.

Paradoxically, men in prison tended to speak of their preference for a lack of control through sleep, but also through complete control of their bodies (as seen in Chapter 3). The key space for many men, in terms of controlling their lives and bodies and making use of their time in prison, was the vital space of the gymnasium.

Masculine Sporting Spaces

The gym and sporting activities featured regularly in participants' narratives about their experiences of imprisonment, and very often in positive terms, with participants speaking of it as one of their favourite places in the prison, and often talking positively about staff members in the gym; some participants spoke of wanting even more gym time. Prisoners had access to two different areas of gym work, weights and fitness, and it was not unusual for participants to speak of favouring one area over the other (it was explained to me that doing both could strip an individual of the strength that they built up in doing weights). The space of the gym itself was sometimes referred to as being different from the rest of the prison:

Logan: The gym, it's like, when you're in the gym you're in a different zone […]
           I think, it's like…you're getting rid of stress and at the same time you're
           keeping healthy and of course you can have a chat with your friends and

it's sociable, it's like, it's like escapism, you're not really in, when I'm there you don't really feel like you're in jail

Working out and exercise were not restricted to the gym, as some participants spoke of taking part in communal sports and activities such as yoga, doing circuits in their cells or in the segregation unit, or using their time in 'exercise' to run outside. Men chose to take part in such activities for various reasons—some saw it as a means of keeping fit and feeling good (especially in view of their negative perceptions of the impact of the prison diet, as already described). Others found that it helped them sleep better after, or saw it as a means of focusing their thoughts, passing time out of their cell, or relieving stress and frustrations, thus allowing them to take control over their bodies, minds, and spaces. Working out was also seen as a means of 'escaping' the prison:

George: That's all I say to my it's like [...], even when I'm at the gym I say I'm going home, when I'm running I say look I'm going home. I'll be running on the treadmill be thinking I'm going home. They're standing at the gate for you, run. And I just push myself, I say run. I just psyche myself up, if I can't [...] I say look, they're waiting for you, now get on that machine, you'd better run, better run. I say, I talk to myself I say run, run fast as you can, just keep running, don't stop. Like little things, like mad little things, I'm say, look they're gonna come and knock you again you'd better run, they're gonna put [...] and then I start running and then I don't stop until I'm dripping, and then I say you know what, I've made it. I'm gonna stop now...it's like little things, the gym is the focus, ask any prisoner...the gymnasium is the only getaway focus

The results of working out took the form of a visible corporeal reward, and many spoke of the importance of being able to see (and show) their work's results and their ability to achieve something:

Benjamin: Coz actually, I suppose, doing the gym, that's a bit alpha male as well [...] You know people probably do it for yeah, gym, prison, it's just, it's stupid, I mean I'm [X] years old, not 12
Researcher: (laughs) Do people do that a lot in the gym then... [...] ...kind of parading?
Benjamin: Oh yeah, when they finish the session taking their tops off and giving it all that

The interpersonal aspects of the gym were somewhat complicated—some were seen by others to use such spaces to perform their physical masculinity for other men or as a location for socialising, whilst other participants spoke of training as being an individual activity. A number of individuals played a role in encouraging others to take part in the gym and take courses in the gym, building up qualifications that would allow many of them to seek jobs in the fitness sector in the future, so honing masculine physiques in order to gain a legitimate male occupation, again distorting heteronormative specifications of gaze (see Chapter 3).

The gym and sport provided sources of gendered discourse and display that could shore up a sense of self in prison but also help shape a life outside. It is thought provoking to note that those men who were classed as vulnerable were only able to access limited facilities and spaces due to potential risks, and thus were excluded from another forum for legitimate masculine performance. It is also compelling to see how exercise is frequently referred to as 'working out', thereby linking it firmly to another discursive marker of masculinity: work (see Chapter 4).

Reflexive Note

Contrary to some suggestions in the literature (see King and Liebling 2008; Sloan and Wright 2015), I spent my fieldwork in the prison with keys. This gave me access to many spaces that were unavailable to the majority of men in the prison, such as 'clean' spaces (staff-only zones where prisoners were never allowed), the segregation wing, the medical centre, the OMU, and so on. This was a very strange experience, as it sometimes required me to challenge prisoners who wished to follow me through a gate, and therefore placed me in a difficult position of power over the men. In essence, I had subverted my own gender by having greater access than most men to the restricted spaces of the prison. I think this was one of the aspects of the prison research experience that affected me the most, because the responsibility of having keys, and the hugely symbolic and gendered nature, gave me an image and a power that I did not expect, and actually did not want. At the same time, it was fascinating to be able to see how men behaved differently in different spaces.

Different spaces in the prison evoked different feelings. Crewe et al. (2014) has spoken of different areas in prisons being seen as 'emotion zones', such as the visiting room, but on a more subconscious level, I observed different feelings in different spaces. The newer wings of the prison tended to be much more pleasant to be in: the men were more relaxed, there was more light and visibility across the wing, and they felt somewhat 'safe'. Other locations were less positive. I vividly remember walking through another of the prison buildings and looking through the bars into another wing, filled in shadow, where a lone figure stood at the gate watching, but not clear to see. The place felt sinister, as did the medical wing and the segregation unit—none of which had much natural light, and all of which—upon personal reflection—felt like spaces of sadness and without hope. They also aligned most closely with extreme popular cultural representations of prisons in films like *Shutter Island* or *The Shawshank Redemption* (see also Jewkes 2014 regarding the importance of darkness and light in penal understandings). In addition, all the spaces within the prison seemed to be occupied by—and guarded by—male figures. In every space there was at least one conspicuously masculine staff presence, and in a number of instances that individual also used my femininity and naivety as a tool for masculine self-escalation. It was as if a feminine presence made those spaces even more masculine.

Summary

Ultimately, all spaces are gendered, albeit to different degrees. Spain argues that 'women and men are spatially segregated in ways that reduce women's access to knowledge and thereby reinforce women's lower status relative to men's. "Gendered spaces" separate women from knowledge used by men to produce and reproduce power and privilege' (1992: 3). When applied to the prison, this can take on a completely different appearance. Prison reduces a prisoner's access to spaces, and certain spaces are only made available to those that the prison institution has deemed 'worthy' (e.g. trustworthy cleaners, those who have proven themselves to be 'good' through achieving 'enhanced' status on the Incentives and Earned Privileges [IEP] scale, get access to more time in the gym, etc.).

This also has the impact of enhancing the individual's visibility (and therefore masculine status) within the prison.

With this in mind, prison actually places most prisoner men into the realm of the female—it restricts access to spaces and areas of power and knowledge, and therefore personal control over their use of time, which Chapter 4 has established already to be of consequence, in the same way that male spaces act upon women outside prison. Indeed:

> A condition and consequence of women's subordinate position in the public sphere, and their ascribed domestic role in the private sphere, is that of significantly inhibiting their power to make decisions about their own time and that of others. (Odih 1999: 22)

This, in turn, affects how men are able to use the spaces available to them, and their experiences of using such spaces (and why this often results in a hypermasculine use of spaces that are accessible, such as areas used to demonstrate corporeal masculinities, or the sexualisation of spaces such as through decoration with 'Page 3' pictures).

The different spaces made available to men (the cell, the wing, the education department, work spaces, etc.) are all used for different masculine demonstrations and performances as a result of the different audiences present in each space, and due to the fact that power is structured differently in each space as a result of them not being accessible to all. Those who have access to more spaces that could be seen to have masculine credentials (i.e. restricted spaces) are able to escape a degree of feminisation that occurs to those for whom spatiality is restricted. Cleaning jobs, for instance, grant prisoners access to different places, which, in turn, grants them a degree of power and status, and thus access to a variety of masculine credentials (i.e. trust, respect, money, time used in a productive way, etc.). Yet overall, all men serving time in prison are restricted by the very fact that they have been sentenced to prison, and thus had spatial restrictions imposed upon them. In actuality, if one considers the range of penalties available to punish men across the world, what lies in common with them all is that the more serious the punishment, the greater the spatial restrictions imposed. Some would see this in terms of 'freedom'—it is clear that such notions of freedom are, at the fore, highly gendered:

Sebastian: So I could never relax in here really, whichever way you look at it, I could have, you know, I don't know, you could give me all this food that I'm wanting or widescreen telly or whatever in my cell, and I'll still not be relaxed coz at the end of the day I'm in prison and I don't want to be here

The use of masculinity as an analytical lens adds a new dimension to the consideration of prisoners' spatial experiences, which rarely frame such notions in terms of gender, thereby highlighting how identity is inherently linked to individuals' access to, and use of, masculine spaces. Where individuals are not able to access such signifiers, negative manifestations of prison-based masculinity have more opportunity for use, thereby highlighting the importance of maintaining individuals' access to spaces of masculinity.

Such management of individual elements of discomfort and harm cannot alter the abiding influence of incarceration itself upon the individual's masculine identity and the impact of having to perform a masculine identity that conforms to the hypermasculine expectations of the prison setting, which often undermines the socially legitimate expectations imposed upon men outside prison. The majority of day-to-day uses of spaces described were for the purpose of reducing the harm of imprisonment, rather than being for any particular proactive purpose—they were to use up otherwise wasted time, avoid the loss of individuality that prisoners often experience, or avoid trouble from other prisoners. It is to the consideration of relationships with others, their importance, and their implications that we now turn.

References

Baer, L. D. (2005). Visual imprints on the prison landscape: A study on the decorations in prison cells. *Tijdschrift voor Economische en Sociale Geografie*, *96*(2), 209–217.

Baer, L. D., & Ravneberg, B. (2008). The outside and inside in Norwegian and English prisons. *Geografiska Annaler: Series B, Human Geography*, *90*(2), 205–216.

Cope, N. (2003). 'It's No Time or High Time': Young offenders' experiences of time and drug use in prison. *The Howard Journal*, *42*(2), 158–175.

Corston, B. J. (2007). *The Corston Report: A report of a review of women with particular vulnerabilities in the criminal justice system.* London: Home Office.

Crewe, B. (2009). *The prisoner society: Power, adaptation, and social life in an English prison.* Oxford, New York: Oxford University Press.

Crewe, B., Warr, J., Bennett, P., & Smith, A. (2014). The emotional geography of prison life. *Theoretical Criminology, 18*(1), 56–74.

Curtis, A. 2014. "'You Have to Cut it off at the Knee': Dangerous Masculinity and SecurityInside a Men's Prison." Men and Masculinities 17:120–46.

Dirsuweit, T. (1999). Carceral spaces in South Africa: A case study of institutional power, sexuality and transgression in a women's prison. *Geoforum, 30*(1), 71–83.

Elger, B. S. (2004). Prevalence, types and possible causes of insomnia in a Swiss remand prison. *European Journal of Epidemiology, 19*, 665–677.

Henderson, C. R. (1911). The cell: A problem of prison science. *Journal of the American Institute of Criminal Law and Criminology, 2*(1), 56–67.

Higate, P. R. (2000). Tough bodies and rough sleeping: Embodying homelessness amongst ex-Servicemen. *Housing, Theory and Society, 17*(3), 97–108.

Ireland, J. L., & Culpin, V. (2006). The relationship between sleeping problems and aggression, anger, and impulsivity in a population of juvenile and young offenders. *Journal of Adolescent Health, 38*, 649–655.

Janssen, J. (2005). Tattoos in prison: Men and their pictures on the edge of society. In B. van Hove & K. Horschelmann (Eds.), *Spaces of masculinities* (pp. 179–192). New York: Routledge.

Jewkes, Y. (2014). 'Punishment in black and white: Penal 'hell-holes', popular media and mass incarceration', *Atlantic Journal of Communication* special issue on 'Reframing Race and Justice in the Age of Mass Incarceration' *22*(1), 42–60.

Jewkes, Y. & Moran, D. (2014, Jan 31). Bad design breeds violence in sterile megaprisons. *The Conversation.* Retrieved November, 2015.

King, R. D., & Liebling, A. (2008). Doing research in prisons. In R. D. King & E. Wincup (Eds.), *Doing research on crime and justice* (2nd ed.). Oxford and New York: Oxford University Press.

Martin, C. (2000). Doing research in a prison setting. In V. Jupp & P. Davies (Eds.), *Doing criminological research* (pp. 215–233). London: Sage.

Odih, P. (1999). Gendered time in the age of deconstruction. *Time and Society, 8*(1), 9–38.

Shalev, S. (2013). *Supermax: Controlling risk through solitary confinement.* Cullompton: Willan Publishing.

Sibley, D., & van Hoven, B. (2009). The contamination of personal space: Boundary construction in a prison environment. *Area, 41*(2), 198–206.

Sloan, J. (2012a). 'You Can See Your Face in My Floor': Examining the function of cleanliness in an adult male prison. *The Howard Journal of Criminal Justice, 51*(4), 400–410.

Sloan, J. (2012b). Cleanliness, spaces and masculine identity in an adult male prison. *Prison Service Journal, 201*, 3–6.

Sloan, J., & Wright, S. (2015). Going in green: Reflections on the challenges of 'getting in, getting on, and getting out' for doctoral researchers. In D. H. Drake, R. Earle, & J. Sloan (Eds.), *The Palgrave handbook of prison ethnography*. Palgrave Macmillan: Basingstoke.

Spain, D. (1992). *Gendered spaces*. Chapel Hill and London: The University of North Carolina Press.

Sykes, G. (1958). *The society of captives: A study of a maximum security prison* (2007th ed.). Princeton, NJ: Princeton University Press.

Van Hoven, B., & Sibley, D. (2008). 'Just duck': The role of vision in the production of prison spaces. *Environment and Planning D: Society and space, 26*(6), 1001.

Warren, J. I., Hurt, S., Booker Loper, A., & Chauhan, P. (2004). Exploring prison adjustment among female inmates: Issues of measurement and prediction. *Criminal Justice and Behaviour, 31*(5), 624–645.

6

Relational Masculinities

It has already been recognised that men are often feminised through the prison experience—having feminine dimensions of time, space, and corporeal spectacle imposed upon them. This also occurs through the very people that a male prisoner comes into contact with on a daily basis, even if those people are men, and even if their behaviours are perceived to be 'hypermasculine'.

Within the prison, 'normal' gendered relational dimensions are disrupted—there are very few women against whom to juxtapose one's masculine identity. For those staff members who are female, many are positioned in the male guise through being 'spectators', having power over other men and even dressed to follow masculine patterns and uniformity similar to the military. These women are infused with power over men in prison, placing men into the feminised, dominated position (see also Crewe 2006a). It falls to other men and such 'masculinised' women to provide the spectrum of gender against which men can position themselves and be positioned by other men.

The prisoner as part of a social group or 'prisoner community' (Hayner and Ash 1939: 362) has dominated sociological studies of imprisonment for decades. Clemmer's study on an American penitentiary in the 1930s,

© The Editor(s) (if applicable) and The Author(s) 2016
J.A. Sloan, *Masculinities and the Adult Male Prison Experience*,
DOI 10.1057/978-1-137-39915-1_6

The Prisoner Community, considered both the social aspects of the prisoner community and more intimate relationships between individuals such as cellmates. On the wider social scale, Clemmer looked at the prisoner community in terms of social relations and communication—particularly argot, which he recognised to have masculine attributes: 'argot, such as exists in a prison will usually be found in other all-male groups, as among hoboes and in armies' (1958: 89). The importance of the individual is also highlighted by Clemmer, who found that 95 % of prisoners were more interested in themselves than in other prisoners (1958: 123), a notion that emerged from my own interviews. With regard to personal identity (and thus the gendered nature of self), there is a tangled interplay between the individual and the community or group within which that individual is situated.

When considered in the light of theories of masculinity, this makes sense—particularly if we consider men to use other men, crime, and interactions with women as means through which to prove their *own* masculine identities (i.e. to prove their masculinities to themselves—see Messerschmidt 1993; Kimmel 1994; Connell 2005). Sykes and Messinger (1960) argue that a cohesive inmate society provides a group for the individual *to align himself with* for support, in addition to providing a shared belief system, a sense of independence, and an institutionalised value ascribed to the ability to withstand the harsh prison environment, shaping his masculine identity.

As it is, the notion of relationships of solidarity within the prison is a complex issue (Irwin 1970), particularly with respect to the modern prison estate, which has been argued on the one hand to be much more individualistic in nature (Crewe 2007), and on the other often suffers (particularly in the USA or South Africa, for instance) from the effects of exaggerated forms of masculine socialisation and common groupings when they take the form of potentially violent and harmful prison gangs (see Jacobs 1974; Fong 1990). Phillips makes note of the fact that such solidarity, when based upon racial or ethnic foundations, can create a resentment among those who are not included (Phillips 2008: 320), and it is important to recognise that this has implications for masculine groupings. In addition, Goffman has pointed out that the process of socialisation can in itself be seen to be painful and have implications (such as feelings of 'contamination'—see also Sibley and van Hoven 2009) regarding an individual's control over his prison experience and gendered self and identity management (1961: 28). Such 'contamination' feelings generally stem from how an individual views others relative to notions of audiences of value, and how they define their interactions.

Labelling Prison Relationships

Participants' detailed narratives tended to identify such interactions with other prisoners in a convoluted light, with even the very labels applied to interactions being distinct to the prison setting. Inter-prisoner relationships were situational, often with people that participants would not be friends with outside prison:

Oliver: Not that I've got anything against anyone, but I...it's only because I'm in prison that I talk to them [...] That's why. Because we would never have met and I doubt, you know...they're not my kind of people most of them, but, yeah, it's funny because you act like you're all friends, well...don't act like you're all friends but...with certain people, act like we're friends but...then say if they left me their number or something I wouldn't...I wouldn't phone 'em, there's people that gave me their number in here, for when I get out, and I've just, I've took it and I've just ripped it up and put it in the bin—I haven't told 'em that, but... [...] No they're not, I don't know what it is, prison friends I suppose, buddies, whatever. It's hard to explain

Gabriel: ...I've met some real good guys in prison and all [...] Real sound salts of the earth, you know what I mean...I ain't ever going to see them again so you don't bother do ya... [...] ...and you ent, you ent going to see them again so it's pointless, you know what I mean so people are just acquaintances

This was due in part, I learned, to others' prisoner/criminal identities and the potential risks they brought to individuals' non-prisoner identity performances. With this in mind, inter-prisoner relationships were generally characterised as being transient and temporary (a notion recognised in the context of the female prison estate by Greer [2000: 449]) with a limited number having the potential to be genuine friendships—their value was, as a result, highly situational. Those that were seen to be genuine were, in part, a result of personal affinities between individuals, but also due to an investment in the other individual, be that an investment of time or openness and trust (as was noted to occur in therapeutic communities with established positive audiences, for example).

The transient nature of this audience that matters is apparent. In addition, some relationships were seen to be potentially and actually negative for individuals to become engaged in within the prison setting. The potential for harm from others was seen to add a defining feature to inter-prisoner relationships as a whole, in that many spoke of the individualistic nature of associations within prison:

Zachary: No I don't think you can ever have friends in prison [...] Just because um... no matter what they say, everybody's got their own agenda I think in prison, everyone's got a little, they must have a little agenda and um maybe I'm just paranoid but...and we are kind of mistrustful people, people from our experiences anyway um...but people just tend to be like looking out for themselves more than anything, so you can get close to a person and they can watch your back to a certain extent but...when um, you know, you find yourself in trouble it's you on your own most of the time

Thus, participants tended to characterise 'true' friends as having elements such as personal affinities, shared histories or backgrounds, a degree of loyalty and investment, an acceptance of friends being able to associate with their family, choice and trust; thereby distancing them to a degree from the 'harmful' prisoner identity. In truth, a number of participants emphasised the fact that many of their friends outside were non-criminal. Prisoners were an audience that mattered in a particular time and space, but generally not in the long term.

Trust was a key element that was often seen to be missing in inter-prisoner relationships, and certain interactions were recognised as not being genuine (see also Crewe 2009: 432) and lacking in openness:

Cameron: Mates not friends [...] Uh, I, because I've only met them in prison I don't know them, even though we've spent a year or two on the wings together... I don't know...the person, I know the character but not the person [...]

> But um…as far as trust goes with these mates, sort of like 90 % I'd trust em, there's that little 10 % is the doubt, and that's only because I met them in prison, I don't know them out there […] And I'm aware that in prison, prisoners do get through their sentence by putting on a brave front

The notion of a 'brave front' (as discussed in Chapter 3) is both masculine and is indicative of underlying fearfulness and processes of performance. Although there was debate as to whether true friendships could occur within the prison setting, and though some did use the term 'friend' to describe interactions, many spoke in less emotive and connected terms (whilst also implying a greater degree of masculinity—perhaps as a tool to add distance from the more emotive quality of friendships). Such terms included 'brothers' (see also Phillips [2008: 319]); 'mates', found by others to be based upon a 'long acquaintanceship', and to be forms of 'defensive alliances as well as reciprocal supports against the deprivations of imprisonment' (Morris and Morris 1963: 224); or, most commonly, 'associates', as recognised by a multitude of prison researchers over the decades (Clemmer [1958: 139]; Flanagan [1980: 154]; Greer [2000]; Liebling and Arnold [2002: 358]; and Crewe [2005a: 473]). Participants were clear in their recognition of a distinction between associates and friends:

Benjamin: It's like well…I think the best way to describe it is, obviously you get work colleagues, it's just people that surround you at a time that you've got to have contact with, really, that's the way I describe it […] It's people you wouldn't necessarily to, you know, go out the way to obviously to you know have any form of relationship with, it's like work, you know, associates, you know it's the environment we're in

Outside masculine signifiers such as the world of work are drawn upon inside the prison in order to attempt to normalise the prison experience (see also Sloan 2015). The nature of relationships in prison is difficult to define—they can be highly situational, transient, and temporary, and there is often seen to be limited potential for making true friends as opposed to 'brothers', 'mates', or 'associates'. This is generally a result of the lack of trust or openness within the prison setting, but although this was emphasised, and although relationships were sometimes seen to be 'work-like', there were references to the potential for, and existence of, friendships, based upon shared affinities, investments, loyalty, and trust, and contingent upon individual prisoners and their circumstances. The key role, however, was that of a situational audience.

Such audience/performer dimensions occurred under a number of different settings. Prisoners would work out and train with other prisoners (sharing in corporeal masculinities), would eat with them—eating and food is recognised to have gendered dimensions to it (Julier and Lindenfeld 2005; Sobal 2005; McPhail et al. 2012)—(although this was by no means a routine occurrence across participants), spend association time with them, borrow and lend (sharing in consumer masculinities— see Crewe 2009: 277), and so on. Of additional importance was the role of other men in prison as a tool in further performances, against which to position one's own masculinity and masculine identity markers. This generally occurred through highlighting positions of difference.

Differentiation

Differentiation is quite a prominent theme within the prison setting— prisoners tend to position themselves relative to others and their 'negative' or 'failing' masculinities, be those other prisoners whom they see to be failing the prisoner collective with regard to perceived imposed obligations, or other prisoners whom they see to be vulnerable, weak, or harmful. Such differentiation allows a level of individuality to be claimed by the prisoner (who is essentially taking control over his identity and how he wished to be viewed relative to other men), and allows for the negotiation of negative identity labels. Prisoners often differentiate themselves from others whom they see as being distanced from the criminal world—non-criminals—thereby positing themselves somewhat negatively. On occasion, the men I spoke to distanced themselves from negative associations they had on the outside, such as criminal friends/ peers who they felt would subsequently impede personal development towards a non-criminal/drugs-free masculine identity: in this instance, it is clear to see a shift in the 'audience that matters' to the individual, and its potential to impact upon desistance and reintegration.

In the prison, the men I spoke to differentiated themselves from other prisoners, generally in the negative—crimes they had committed weren't as bad as *others'*; the way an individual performed his masculine identity was nowhere near as staged or negative as *others'*; individuals made use of their time, rather than wasting it as *others* did; and so on. Such differentiation can be manipulated to suit the audience. As such, differentiation processes highlight the flexibility of individual prisoners' associations and performances, with the potential to signal different elements of self to different people at different times, depending on who matters then.

Clearly, the relationships that prisoners have with each other are complicated. Relationships could be characterised as positive, negative, and neutral; however, the most unusual point was the fact that prisoners apply distinctive labels to such interactions, seemingly avoiding indicators of emotional connection or closeness in the majority of cases. This may well be for the reason that prisoners would find it difficult to put the practice of differentiation from the prisoner identity that they see in others into action if they could be identified as friends—friends tend to be individuals with shared attributes to ourselves. The ability to differentiate from the prisoner collective with all its associated negative attributes and characteristics was critical, and ties in well with Douglas' notion of 'danger-beliefs' whereby:

> certain moral values are upheld and certain social rules defined by beliefs in dangerous contagion, as when the glance or touch of an adulterer is held to bring illness to his neighbour or his children. (1966: 3)

If we apply this concept to prisoner identity, it is arguable that the prisoner identity could be seen to be contagious through proximity—this idea could be seen to manifest itself in the differentiation and avoidance behaviours seen regarding cleanliness. The avoidance of expressions of relationships of closeness can be seen to be another mechanism through which prisoners implement individualisation and differentiation processes and attempt to manage the contagiousness of the prisoner identity, instead opting for labels of association to apply to positive interactions with other prisoners.

Where positive relationships did exist, these tended to be based upon similarities between individuals that went beyond the prisoner label and again differentiated them from others. Such characteristics included family or friendship ties that originated outside prison, interests in music or religion, or shared distinctive experiences within the prison setting, such as therapeutic environments. These tended to represent elements of openness and trust, which were lacking in the majority of interactions within the prison, although even in positive interactions individuals tended to be guarded and apply protective fronts. Other relationships that were seen in a positive light tended to be those that could either affirm or improve an individual's masculine 'credentials' within the prison, such as providing protection or help to those weaker individuals, learning skills that would afford them independence within the prison, or, in some cases, providing relationships of emotional support:

Bailey:	I think people are lying when they say they don't make friends in jail so…I do, I like people so
Researcher:	Mmhmm, so what is it about the guys you get on with that makes them friends?
Bailey:	Um…well you just help people out ent it, somebody's probably on a downer one day and you'll go and sit with him and then you next week you'll be a bit down and he'll come and sit with you and we'll have a coffee, PlayStation, and, um, you just help people out don't you […] It's good support isn't it

This was rare, as it could be perceived as a sign of weakness and would undermine the differentiation process, and where such relationships of trust did occur they would still be managed to some extent in order to retain a degree of toughness.

Negative interactions tended to centre on elements of harm—a number of prisoners spoke of their experiences of threatening or harmful behaviours from others. Often, prisoners would attempt to normalise such experiences or observations within the prison context and thus situate such harms within the prison and its spatial context (see Chapter 5), rather than being linked to them as an individual 'victim' who could be seen to be weak. Many spoke of the means through which they altered their behaviours in order to negotiate the risk of such harms from others, and the lack of trust experienced between prisoners was inherent in the negative relationships experienced and the resultant negotiative behaviours. Negative relationships existed where individuals exerted too much or too little control—too much control over others in the form of harmful and manipulative behaviours, or too little control where individuals failed either to differentiate themselves from the prisoner collective (and thus be seen as trustworthy or have non-prison affinities with others), or where individuals failed to take control over their performed identities as men and thus move away from a 'weak' identity (i.e. not conform to the expectations of the prisoner collective). As such, relationships between prisoners in prison required a delicate balance between being situated within the prisoner collective with its associated risks and contagiousness, or being situated out of that group and thus out of the protective solidarity that still remains to some degree. Yet in many instances, it is the internalised expectations that an individual places on himself in response to the audience community around him that frames an individual's actions.

Harmful Masculine Interactions

The performance of gender can sometimes result in extreme and harmful behaviours: violence is high in communicative value (Crawley and Crawley 2008). Thus violence can be an easy way to display the self relative to, and to, others, as well as heighten personal visibility. The majority of participants had either directly experienced or observed such incidents:

Oscar: [...] see you look surprised, to me it doesn't, doesn't bother me... [...] you know I think, phh, s, someone gets cut up you're just like oh right [...] Yeah it's, it's that bad, you know, like oh someone got hot water down over on [X] wing, oh, ok, not like oh, really! Someone got hot watered? Bloody hell, was he alright? Nah. It's just yeah whatever mate, who cares...because it's such a normal thing

The negative behaviours of some prisoners impacted upon the majority in terms of behaviours, interactions, and reactions (in this instance, normalisation of this particular experience placed the individual within the "safety" of the prisoner collective). Participants spoke of having to manage their interactions with others in order to avoid conflicts with people who might take things the wrong way, or about having to lock their doors when they left their cells in order to avoid being victimised. Although many spoke of not caring about the views of others—not valuing that audience—this opinion tended to be undermined when considering the fact that many participants spoke of the ways in which they managed themselves and their interactions with others in order either to avoid confrontation/victimisation, or to manage how others saw them as individuals:

Noah: A lot of it's moving about, yeah coz obviously groups of people, people
          gathering, [...] and uh, you find that's where a lot of stuff kicks off, you
          know [...] And uh...so it's quite a...you know, you have to be on guard,
          yeah, coz, you don't know what's going, even though you do nothing, you
          know you don't know if someone's took umbrage to something or someone
          else is, you know, or, you know you've had an argument with someone down
          the line [...] And so it's always, you know, them times that you have to be
          on guard when you're...being moved, you know coz there's no staff about.
          And I suppose they're the most apprehensive sort of times, to me

On a wider level, too, prisoners who undermined this idea that 'we're all in the same boat' and differentiated themselves from the prison community too much (such as feeling that their personal problems were more serious than others') were seen negatively. Prisoners who overexaggerated individualism and differentiation in personal narratives, or who were seen to be complaining too much, borrowing unnecessarily, getting into debt, or failing to maintain personal hygiene (see Sloan 2012a, b) were all spoken of negatively by participants. In a similar vein, participants spoke in negative terms of individuals who bullied or took advantage of more vulnerable prisoners, in addition to those who failed to show an acceptable level of courtesy and respect to others (such as through cleanliness or keeping noise to an acceptable level)—people wanted to be audiences that mattered to some degree, as this would shape others' behaviours in line with their own values. In some instances this was seen to come with maturity, with younger prisoners being criticised for failing to adhere to such expectations. Participants recognised that inter-prisoner relationships were less volatile in adult prisons compared to young offender institutions, where there was much more violence and a need to prove one's masculine self (see also Jackson 2002).

Despite its communicative value (Crawley and Crawley 2008), violence as a whole was seen to be something to try to avoid within the adult male prison setting, having the potential to have an adverse effect upon sentence length, although at the same time, individuals sometimes referred to having to be able to prove themselves capable of committing violence if the occasion came, in order to prevent personal victimisation and demonstrate physical hardness. There was an unwritten code of behaviour with respect to relationships with others—such a code referred to coping with incarceration and an all-male context where escape and finding other contexts for interaction are very limited.

Negative interactions with other prisoners changed the way that individuals behaved and performed their identities, often being the reason behind putting up an emotional barrier to others and not being fully open (which, in turn, fostered a feeling of tension and distrust within the prison and created a perpetual cycle (see also Crewe 2009) . In addition, participants spoke of feeling that they could not respond to such threats negatively as they wished to demonstrate that they had changed their behaviours and ways of doing masculinity (see West and Zimmerman 1987; Messerschmidt 1993) in order to be considered for release or privileges. The staff audience mattered, not least due to its extreme power over how a male prisoner is seen by those of real emotional value to him, such as his family. Having to police their external identities created stress, both internalised and impacting upon their relations with others. In this way, it is understandable that—in line with Sykes' pain of the deprivation of security (1958: 76)—living with prisoners was seen to be one of the key negatives of incarceration:

Jude: […] you know it was just, just a personality clash, just didn't get on, you know, I said something, he disagreed with it, he said something, I disagreed with it, and that's, and that's a big pressure, you know, when you're in with somebody and that much pressure's coming from it, that much…you know that's, that's another sentence in itself, that's another punishment, you know […]

Harrison: Coz I've never been like that, I'd never do drugs and things like that, so to be around that's not very nice, plus you get them all walking around asking for burn,[1] ah, 'have you got a fag, have you got this, have you got that, have you got tinfoil' d'you know what I mean, it's not very nice. What else is there?

Researcher: So you don't like being asked to, for that kind of stuff?

Harrison: Yeah, it's horrible, because you can just be sitting in your cell doing something and next thing you turn around and there's people like, obviously not very nice looking, they've got no teeth and they're all thin and look just horrible, asking you for things to do drugs with and it's like, nah. Coz I'm comfortable with everything, I don't mind them doing it, let them get on with what they're doing init, but when they're coming into my space, like making me feel uncomfortable, that's when I don't like it

Staff

Another layer of complexity and masculinity is added to the prisoner's experience when considering the interactions between prisoners and staff. The impacts of relationships between staff and prisoners have been widely discussed within both the academic literature and on a wider policy scale (Walmsley et al. 1992; Woolf and Tumin 1991: 1.149). On a more sociological basis, such relationships have been seen to be significant to the prison experience for many years, both for instrumental and normative reasons (Liebling and Price 1999: 22), although it is recognised that staff find getting the appropriate social distance between themselves and prisoners, and the balance between friendliness and friendship, somewhat tricky and individually dependent (Crawley 2004: 106–107), in part as a result of similarities between prisoners and officers in terms of the 'narrowness of the socio-economic (and moral) divide between themselves and prisoners' (2004: 122)—arguably, this can extend to masculinity too. As Goffman notes, the relationships between staff and prisoners in total institutions can be complicated for staff members:

---

[1] 'Burn' is tobacco.

In an effort to frustrate these visibly self-destructive acts, staff members may find themselves forced to manhandle these patients, creating an image of themselves as harsh and coercive just at the moment when they are attempting to prevent someone from doing to himself what they feel no human being should do to anyone. (1961: 83)[2]

The relationship between staff and prisoner has been noted to have changed within the late-modern prison estate, however, with the shift in power away from uniformed staff working directly with prisoners, upwards towards more centralised and managerial staff members (Crewe 2007). This goes hand in hand with the process of individualisation that is occurring with regard to the social interactions between prisoners themselves (Crewe 2007: 259, 273), although Morris and Morris argue that this is less relevant, as the uniformed prison officers actually execute such decisions, and thus embody authority (1963: 264). This has potential implications for a shift in the dynamics of relationships between prisoners and staff and the degree to which they can be said to have direct power over the prisoner's sentence and experience—officers are now 'not seen as *embodying* the system of power so much as *implementing* it' (Crewe 2007: 261).

Yet it must be remembered that staff are still an audience for prisoners' masculine performances—and an audience with a high degree of institutional power behind them. In addition to recognising the importance of the custodian-prisoner relationship and its associated 'trades' (1958: 57) and discretion in the maintenance of order in the absence of complete power over prisoners, Sykes goes on to link some of his suggested pains of imprisonment to the roles of prison staff. The deprivations of liberty, goods, and services and heterosexual relationships (and the promotion of personal security) are all enforced by staff members, but of greatest concern is the fact that the deprivation of autonomy has direct implications for a prisoner's masculine identity (see Crewe 2006a: 415) by infantilising and feminising him:

The frustration of the prisoner's ability to make choices and the frequent refusals to provide an explanation for the regulations and commands descending from the bureaucratic staff involve a profound threat to the

---

[2] An interesting choice of words to use the term 'manhandle', yet this is symbolic of such interactions between prisoners and staff, and highlights some of the issues raised when female officers step into such a masculine role (Crewe 2006a).

prisoner's self image because they reduce the prisoner to the weak, helpless, dependent status of childhood. (Sykes 1958: 75)

Such control (and its potential abuse) over the fate of inmates can have implications in terms of the lack of trust prisoners can experience with reference to staff members (Winfree et al. 2002: 229), and the negative perceptions of a lack of openness (Liebling and Price 1999: 20). Liebling and Arnold found the dimension of 'staff-prisoner relationships' that they investigated to be most highly correlated with dimensions of respect, humanity, fairness, trust, and support regarding staff actions and attitudes (2004: 239).

The negative aspects and implications of prisoner-staff relationships have been regularly acknowledged, particularly with respect to the negative impacts such interactions can have upon inter-prisoner relationships due to their undermining of the prisoner code (Sykes and Messinger 1960; Morris and Morris 1963; Winfree et al. 2002). Platek observed of the group assigned the non-'man' status of 'mug': 'the most odious of "mugs" are prison functionaries. A "man" may have no contact whatever with a jailer' (1990: 462), with masculine identities thus being shaped by the manner of associations occurring between prisoners and staff (and vice versa). Some prisoners also avoid contact with prison officers (and other prisoners) in order to become 'mentally and materially independent' in a process referred to as 'isolationism' (Grapendaal 1990: 347). As Wheeler points out, 'the inmate who values friendship among his peers and also desires to conform to the staff's norms faces a vivid and real role conflict' (1961: 704). Indeed, which audience should take priority and be of higher value?

The gendered nature of staff-prisoner relationships has been acknowledged to a degree within academic literature—Sim has recognised that prison staff can provide another source of masculine expectation for inmates regarding the performance of their gendered identity, thus imposing a degree of identity pressure in addition to other prisoners (Sim 1994: 102—see also Jewkes 2002: 141). My research study also brought to light the fact that relationships between prisoners and members of staff had a key influence upon individuals' experiences of imprisonment. In addition to being responsible for mundane domestic responsibilities, situating prison as a 'quasi-domestic sphere' (Crawley 2004: 130), staff members were also seen as having wider responsibilities such as welfare and security. Similar to prisoners, the hypermasculine expectations were in tension with the somewhat feminised reality. Participants spoke of there being greater potential for problems and confrontations when staff were not visible or present—staff members had control over prisoners, a fact that many prisoners (albeit appreciating its implications in terms of personal safety) often resented due to it enforcing a state of emasculating dependence:

Kai: Well you can't do what you want [...] You just can't do, you can't get up in the morning, put your clothes on and walk down the shop...get yourself a newspaper or, or, they, the worst thing about it is you cannot do what you wanna do [...] You know you're confined to do what they want you to do [...] You know and I know outside...you live by, you live by the laws of the land and all that but you can do what you want to do, you've got them choices to do what you wanna do, I think in here the worst thing about jail is not having your choices...your freedom to do what you want, d' you know what I mean, for me that is the worst thing

It was acknowledged that staff were often very busy and lacked time, which meant that some processes within the prison were highly time-consuming or delayed with direct knock-on implications for prisoners, re-emphasising their lack of independence or control over their own lives and sentence progression:

Noah: [...] you know it's like I've been waiting for three, four months now for me parole reports...now to me that's an important thing, but to them it's oh right, yeah, don't worry, it'll be done...yeah but when? You know this has got to be back, back, so they don't really take on board how, what the effect of these things have on people so obviously if, if you ask them to do something, I've seen, yeah, you know if I come and ask you to do something for me, oh, you know can you sort this out for me please, I'd sooner say, you say to me right, I'll have a look at it, but I'm not sure if I'll get it done. Whereas they will go, yep, no problems, and when you come back to them, oh I gave that, I give, give that to so and so, yeah alright, you know passing the buck. So obviously that starts to make me agitated. What you playing at? I've asked you to do something simple...if you couldn't do it you should have just told me you couldn't do it and I could have gone to someone else that could have done

Staff were appreciated if they helped prisoners to achieve their targets without such delays, or if they were seen to be helping prisoners to get through the system—there appeared to be a distinction between 'prison staff as individuals' and 'prison staff as the system' (recognised by Liebling and Arnold 2004: 234–239). What was of particular importance to prisoners was the fact that they saw some prison staff as failing to give them the respect—central to their feelings of masculine self—that they felt they deserved:

Oliver:	See maybe it's just me, like em…just the way they'll answer you, yeah and just shut the door, it's just fucking rude for no reason. […] Just coz I'm in prison you don't have to talk to me like I'm, you know, like I'm nothing

Staff obviously had a very difficult role, having to combine discipline with domesticity and care (in a way, having to play out both feminised and masculinised identities in daily interactions), whilst at the same time preserving rapport and security-based suspicions. In addition, the observation of prison staff being there as a job (for career as opposed to care) was used both to criticise staff as well as sympathise with them. When speaking of positive relationships with staff, many participants would refer to individuals or distinct groups such as those in education, the gym, therapy or mental health, or staff working on particular wings. Decent treatment as a whole was valued. At the same time, there were distinct groups who were seen in a particularly negative light, such as psychology (see also Crewe 2007: 261; Sloan and Wright 2015) and management, who would sometimes be used to represent the system. These groups of staff had even more meaningful and effectual control, being able to impose punishments, or write damning psychological reports that could hold a prisoner back years in an indeterminate sentence.

Where men tried to take control and highlight issues, although this might gain kudos from other audiences, participants spoke of the fact that they felt they were seen to be 'whinging'[3] when complaining:

---

[3] In itself, the idea of 'whinging' is referential to a childlike behaviour, thereby highlighting the lack of adult autonomy ascribed to the male prisoner when incarcerated and dependent on others.

Gabriel: I know, it is annoying, what would you do, you know what I mean. And you keep complaining they see you as a pest. [...] You know what I mean, you try to stand up, try to point of views it's like me, you try to stand up for yourself...they see you as a problem. So you can't win in prison [...] You cannot win. You try standing up for yourself and you start putting in complaints and start, you moan about the food and that...they just see you as a control hazard and everything, you know what I mean

Although prisoners and staff had points of conflict, generally with reference to competition for control (most amusingly explained by some in the real-life competition prisoners and staff had to hide and find illegal items), many spoke of the fact that they got on with staff in general. Regardless of the power imbalance, staff members were another type of audience for prisoners to perform their gendered identities for, sometimes with apprehension:

Kai: As much as they're supposed to give you correct, you know, advice and counselling and whatever, they just look at you and think oh you're weak man, do what you, do what you got to do and stuff like that. I don't think there's any of that here, you know, there might be the odd one member of staff who you get on with who you can go to and say listen my head's shot, have you got ten minutes? And who'll just sit there and listen to you d'you know what I mean

Retaining masculine identities for the staff audience, however, was somewhat problematic, as staff were directly aware of prisoners' lack of personal autonomy and control and their power over them. When staff members exerted this power in ways that were seen to be illegitimate, unjust, or too great, participants would speak of their frustration, anger, and dislike of individuals. The implications of such relationships upon individuals' gendered identities and the male prison experience are extensive and potentially volatile in terms of prisoner responses to imprisonment, the prison system, and prison staff as a whole. Such relationships with staff clearly emphasise the importance of control within masculine configurations—*control over oneself* and *control over others*—both within the prison, resulting from the enforced processes of competition and masculine performances of dominance; and on the outside, in terms of retaining control over one's family life and non-prisoner identity signifiers.

Reflexive Note

How I interacted with, and related to, the men and women I met in the prison setting has shaped me for years after. Having never spent a prolonged period in a prison prior to this, it became apparent that the job of working in a prison is fraught with difficulties, stresses, and strains, and is highly intensive when it comes to emotional labour. In addition, the men who are serving time in the prison and who agreed to talk to me were all very polite, insightful, and often intelligent men. 'Normal' men who you might pass by in the street, or who might be a friend or family member, not the 'monsters' they are made out to be in modern press. Even being familiar with the tactics of the media, and the politics and stigma applied to deviant men, it was a shock to the system to see so many similarities between the men I met in the prison and the men I valued in my own life. I met no monsters, just men who had done some monstrous things.

The way those men related to me was compelling. Rarely was I treated with hostility—there was only one man I met who even challenged me in terms of asking why he should help me, what difference it would really make, and subsequently mocking me in front of others (thereby using me as an effective tool to show his dominance and power-claiming abilities—see Chapter 2). He was the only man who actually frightened me— not for his performances, but for his clear intelligence. I did not know what he had done to get there, but being on the lifer wing, it was clearly on the more serious side of the crimes that had been committed.

In general, I was met and spoken to with respect and friendliness. As noted earlier, some men took me under their wing and were quite protective of me:

Elliot: As long as you feel safe and secure
Researcher: Oh I do, I do
Elliot: That's good
Researcher: I do, yeah, everyone, everyone looks out for me (laughs)
Elliot: Oh of course yeah, if anyone gave you lip they'd be […] the guy who's giving you lip

Many chatted to me on the wings, greeting me with some degree of affection (and potentially, wing ownership!). Even for these men, I was a useful mechanism to show heterosexuality and the ability to dominate and protect. I was used as a tool through which the men could perform their masculine identities for the benefit of those watching—the other men on the wing were the obvious 'audience that mattered' in these interactions, but when alone, that audience shifted to a more internalised watcher, and became much less demonstrative of masculine signifiers, it being a much easier process to be seen as a 'man' in a 1:1 situation with a woman, where the gender dichotomy is much more normalised. Such clear shifts in how men performed in different settings for different audiences and different genders was clearly apparent (which would have been lost without placing my own gendered self into the frame).

Summary

This chapter adds to the existing academic debate regarding relationships in prison through the detailed consideration of the importance of masculinity as the central tenet in such interactions. Whereas great consideration has been given to the manifestation and implications of relationships with prisoners and staff, this is rarely seen through the lens of the men's masculine selves and how these identities are shaped as a result of such interactions (which links back to the dimensions of spectacle and spectator in Chapter. 3), and as a result of this highly present male audience. The importance of the male collective as an audience for gendered behaviours and the negotiation of individuals' personal masculinities was evident in interviews, as was the harmful nature of the prisoner identity upon the structure and stability of friendships and interactions in prison. The types of men that individuals wanted to become (i.e. non-prisoners) placed other prisoners as risks to individuals' abilities to differentiate and distinguish themselves from such negative masculine signifiers—friends tended to be seen as those individuals who had scope beyond the prison and thus transcended the prison institution as an audience.

The men could clearly be seen to change their personal performances of self, according to the audience at the time. Such relational signifiers of masculine self, extending from outside the prison, could regularly be referred to as a source of differentiation from the prisoner collective, and thus provide a means through which to assert one's masculine independence and individuality.

Relationships are a powerful means through which individuals are able to shape and perform their masculinities. This occurs both in positive ways, through who they want to be seen to be in the present and the future; and in the negative, in terms of who they do not want to be seen as, and how they must undergo identity management in order to restrict the degree of harm they experience. Such identity management generally requires individuals to distance themselves both from illegitimate masculine performativity (particularly if they wish to achieve legitimate future masculine identities), and from situations in which they may be assessed as being weak or vulnerable (and thus potentially having to resort to such illegitimate means in order to assert toughness and hardness). It is to the concept of vulnerability and its formal management that we now turn.

References

Clemmer, D. (1958). *The prison community* (Newth ed.). New York: Holt, Reinhart and Winston.

Connell, R. W. (2005). *Masculinities* (2nd ed.). Cambridge: Polity Press.

Crawley, E. (2004). *Doing prison work: The public and private lives of prison officers*. Cullompton: Willan Publishing.

Crawley, E., & Crawley, P. (2008). Culture, performance, and disorder: The communicative quality of prison violence. In J. M. Byrne, D. Hummer, & F. S. Taxman (Eds.), *The culture of prison violence*. Boston: Pearson/Allyn and Bacon.

Crewe, B. (2005a). Prisoner society in the era of hard drugs. *Punishment and Society, 7*(4), 457–481.

Crewe, B. (2005b). Codes and conventions: The terms and conditions of contemporary inmate values. In A. Liebling & S. Maruna (Eds.), *The effects of imprisonment*. Cullompton: Willan Publishing.

Crewe, B. (2006a). Male prisoners' orientations towards female officers in an English prison. *Punishment and Society, 8*(4), 395–421.

Crewe, B. (2006b). The drugs economy and the prisoner society. In Y. Jewkes & H. Johnston (Eds.), *Prison readings: A critical introduction to prisons and imprisonment*. Cullompton: Willan Publishing.

Crewe, B. (2006c). Prison drug dealing and the ethnographic lens. *The Howard Journal, 45*(4), 347–368.

Crewe, B. (2007). Power, adaptation and resistance in a late modern men's prison. *British Journal of Criminology, 47*(2), 256–275.

Crewe, B. (2009). *The prisoner society: Power, adaptation, and social life in an English prison.* Oxford, New York: Oxford University Press.

Douglas, M. (1966). *Purity and danger: An analysis of the concepts of pollution and taboo.* London: Routledge and Kegan Paul.

Flanagan, T. J. (1980). The pains of long-term imprisonment: A comparison of British and American perspectives. *British Journal of Criminology, 20*(2), 148–156.

Fong, R. S. (1990). The organizational structure of prison gangs: A Texas case study. *Federal Probation, 54*(1), 36–43.

Goffman, E. (1961). *Asylums: Essays on the social situation of mental patients and other inmates.* Chicago: Aldine Publishing Company.

Grapendaal, M. (1990). The inmate subculture in Dutch prisons. *British Journal of Criminology, 30*(3), 341–357.

Greer, K. R. (2000). The changing nature of interpersonal relationships in a women's prison. *The Prison Journal, 80*(4), 442–468.

Hayner, N. S., & Ash, E. (1939). The prisoner community as a social group. *American Sociological Review, 4*(3), 362–369.

Irwin, J. (1970). *The felon.* New Jersey: Prentice-Hall, Inc.

Jackson, C. (2002). 'Laddishness' as a self-worth protection strategy. *Gender and Education, 14*(1), 37–50.

Jacobs, J. B. (1974). Street gangs behind bars. *Social Problems, 21*(3), 395–409.

Jewkes, Y. (2002). *Captive audience: Media, masculinity and power in prisons.* Cullompton: Willan Publishing.

Julier, A., & Lindenfeld, L. (2005). Mapping men onto the menu: Masculinities and food. *Food and Foodways: Explorations in the History and Culture of Human Nourishment, 13*(1–2), 1–16.

Kimmel, M. S. (1994). Masculinity as homophobia: Fear, shame, and silence in the construction of gender identity. In H. Brod & M. Kaufman (Eds.), *Theorizing masculinities.* Thousand Oaks and London: Sage.

Liebling, A., & Arnold, H. (2002). *Measuring the quality of prison life* (Home Office Findings No. 174). London: Home Office.

Liebling, A., & Arnold, H. (2004). *Prisons and their moral performance.* Oxford and New York: Oxford University Press.

Liebling, A., & Price, D. (1999). *An exploration of staff-prisoner relationships at HMP Whitemoor.* London: Prison Service.

McPhail, D., Beagan, B., & Chapman, G. E. (2012). "I Don't Want to be Sexist But…" denying and re-inscribing gender through food. *Food, Culture and Society, 15*(3), 473–489.

Messerschmidt, J. W. (1993). *Masculinities and crime.* Maryland: Rowman and Littlefield Publishers, Inc.

Morris, T., & Morris, P. (1963). *Pentonville: A sociological study of an English Prison.* London: Routledge and Kegan Paul.

Phillips, C. (2008). Negotiating identities: Ethnicity and social relations in a young offenders' institution. *Theoretical Criminology, 12*(3), 313–331.

Platek, M. (1990). Prison subculture in Poland. *International Journal of the Sociology of Law, 18*, 459–472.

Sibley, D., & van Hoven, B. (2009). The contamination of personal space: Boundary construction in a prison environment. *Area, 41*(2), 198–206.

Sim, J. (1994). Tougher than the rest? Men in prison. In T. Newburn & E. A. Stanko (Eds.), *Just boys doing business? Men, masculinities and crime.* London and New York: Routledge.

Sloan, J. (2012a). 'You Can See Your Face in My Floor': Examining the function of cleanliness in an adult male prison. *The Howard Journal of Criminal Justice, 51*(4), 400–410.

Sloan, J. (2012b). Cleanliness, spaces and masculine identity in an adult male prison. *Prison Service Journal, 201*, 3–6.

Sloan, J. (2015). Masculinity, imprisonment and working identities. In C. Reeves (Ed.), *Experiencing imprisonment: Research on the experience of living and working in carceral institution.* London and New York: Routledge.

Sloan, J., & Wright, S. (2015). Going in green: Reflections on the challenges of 'getting in, getting on, and getting out' for doctoral researchers. In D. H. Drake, R. Earle, & J. Sloan (Eds.), *The Palgrave handbook of prison ethnography.* Palgrave Macmillan: Basingstoke.

Sobal, J. (2005). Men, meat, and marriage: Models of masculinity. *Food and Foodways: Explorations in the History and Culture of Human Nourishment, 13*(1-2), 135–158.

Sykes, G. (1958). *The society of captives: A study of a maximum security prison* (2007th ed.). Princeton, NJ: Princeton University Press.

Sykes, G. M., & Messinger, S. L. (1960). The inmate social system. In R. A. Cloward (Ed.), *Theoretical studies in social organisation of the prison.* New York: Social Science Research Council.

Walmsley, R., Howard, L., & White, S. (1992). *The National Prison Survey 1991 Main Findings* (Home Office Research Study 128). London: HMSO.

West, C., & Zimmerman, D. H. (1987). Doing gender. *Gender and Society, 1*(2), 125–151.

Wheeler, S. (1961). Socialization in correctional communities. *American Sociological Review, 26*(5), 697–712.

Winfree, L. T., Jr., Newbold, G., & Houston Tubb, S., III. (2002). Prisoner perspectives on inmate culture in New Mexico and New Zealand: A descriptive case study. *The Prison Journal, 82*(2), 213–233.

Woolf (Rt Hon Lord Justice) & Tumin (His Honour Judge). (1991). *Prison disturbances April 1990: Report of an inquiry*, Cm 1456. London: HMSO.

7

Vulnerable Masculinities

Men in prison are viewed to be an inherently vulnerable group, yet rarely are the notions of masculinities and vulnerabilities considered together, and even rarer still is a consideration of these interplaying issues on a general level. Whereas consideration of the vulnerability of certain typologies of male prisoner is a regular occurrence within the prison—the bullied prisoner, the self-harming prisoner, the young prisoner, the old and infirm prisoner (labels which go hand in hand with processes of feminisation)—such categorisation ultimately misses both the ways in which men who do not fit into such categorisations also experience vulnerabilities on a daily basis, and the innately masculine natures and implications of such vulnerabilities. Although certain forms of vulnerability are engaged with through formal means (such as group work, offending behaviour programmes, and therapeutic communities), these are limited due to the need for individuals to engage actively with the processes of exposing personal vulnerabilities in formal (and often group) situations where trust could still be seen to be at a premium.

Less attention is given in practice to the day-to-day vulnerabilities of men, manifesting by virtue of their disconnection with 'normal' masculine identity signifiers on the outside, such as families, employment,

© The Editor(s) (if applicable) and The Author(s) 2016
J.A. Sloan, *Masculinities and the Adult Male Prison Experience*,
DOI 10.1057/978-1-137-39915-1_7

independence, and maintaining control—both over themselves through their life course, and over others. Although some forms of control over others on the outside are negative (such as domestic violence), they are still ways through which men are able to situate themselves within patriarchal and masculine systems, and thus provide a means through which to define themselves as men. This is not to say that the facilitation of such controlling and abusive behaviours should be encouraged to promote masculine identity—far from it. Rather, it is crucial to recognise that the means through which men perform and situate themselves within masculine definitions are not always positive, but their total abandonment, rather than the encouragement of (and their replacement with) alternative positive forms of masculine control, results in further problems with respect to the limited legitimate means through which to identify oneself as a man, particularly within the prison.

What is meant by 'vulnerabilities' in the context of masculinities? By vulnerabilities in this context, I refer to the way in which men's masculinities become threatened or put under pressure or tension by virtue of their incarceration. This may be as a result of the pressures to perform certain masculine traits for the benefit of the apparently hypermasculine (yet also feminising) prison sphere, or as a result of self-imposed pressures on the self to act in a certain manner. Although everyone in life is expected to perform in certain ways, rarely are the means through which to achieve a legitimate gendered identity limited in the ways that they can be in prisons, and rarely do such expectations pervade every element of the individual's living space. Even men's cells, whilst on the one hand providing a potential 'safe' or 'neutral' space for the individual when the door is shut, are restrictive in the sense that individuals are limited in what they can do and who they can be whilst inside, and the cells themselves can make some vital statements about men's masculine identities (see Sloan 2012a, b).

It could be argued that the term 'ontological security' would be more appropriate in this case. Jefferson notes that common to all definitions of ontological insecurity (such as the work of Laing [1960] or Giddens [1991]) lies 'a sense of deep-seated uncertainty and instability in the face of perceived or postulated danger' (2010: 389). Although this is a useful way to view the notion of vulnerabilities, what I am concerned with is less 'uncertainty and instability' and less of a 'danger'. Men in prison do not necessarily perceive their masculinities to be in danger—they have plenty of opportunities to act in a masculine fashion if they are willing to do so illegitimately through violence, controlling behaviours, or escaping the situation altogether through substance abuse. They also do not tend to feel uncertain or unstable about their masculinities—few of the men I spoke to actually reflected on their gendered identities, but rather their manifestations in performance such as through families or employment that were denied to or limited for them. Ontological insecurity in the prison setting would arguably extend much broader than the masculine self, to the very identity of the individual, which would apply both to female and male prisoners. Of concern in this chapter, however, are the distinctly masculine aspects of identity that become vulnerable through incarceration.

Masculine Vulnerabilities

When talking to prisoners about their daily lives in prison, it became apparent that *all* the men I spoke to were vulnerable in some way or another, and that those vulnerabilities were rooted within masculine identity. Yes, there were those who had been bullied, those who had been in the care system as children, those who had internalised the pains of imprisonment through self-harm, those who suffered from health issues or had experienced substance abuse problems—but there were also many more who were vulnerable in terms of their lives more generally. Many lacked educational opportunities in their pasts. Many spoke of the vulnerabilities of their identities now they were prisoners, and the implications this may well have on their chances outside the prison. Others spoke of the vulnerabilities of their family lives—the precarious position of their identities as fathers when they may not have had much contact (and particularly not meaningful contact) with their children—or of the implications prison might have upon their bodies, their physical masculinities, and their chances of having children in the future (see Chapter 4).[1]

---

[1] Whilst such vulnerabilities could equally be applied to the female prison population, there is something else that differentiates men and their masculinities and the associated signifiers of gendered self—the importance of others. Men gain their masculine identities not only by self-achievement of status signifiers, but also through the granting of their masculine status by other men (Kimmel 1994). Thus, these signifiers take on even greater externalised importance than for women. Whilst

Such issues spoke directly to the masculinities of the men—in terms of how they could position themselves as men when within the prison, where they lacked opportunities to act out their masculinities legitimately, but also in terms of their 'potential masculinities' in their future lives as they were planning them. Their very identities as men became vulnerable by virtue of their incarceration.

Such theorisations of men suffering such pervasive vulnerabilities do not sit well with common understandings of the prison as an inherently masculine—often hypermasculine—environment. It doesn't make sense. Of course these men can be masculine: by being in prison (and getting through the process), men are able to demonstrate their toughness, their hardness, and their ability to dominate, be that the situation or others around them. And yet, when digging a little deeper, such an environment—by virtue of its overt and overbearing masculinity *and* processes of feminisation running alongside—actually can undermine the masculinities of those within. The aspects of the male prisoner's identity that allowed him to be masculine on the outside (and may even have led up to his prison spell) become denied or highly limited for the individual. He is no longer able to be the 'good' dad easily—his access to his children is limited, both in quality and duration. He is no longer able to be the 'good' partner (or even he bad partner), who displays his masculinity—his access to willing partners is highly limited. He is no longer able to do a full working day—most (closed) prisons are not equipped for individuals to undertake meaningful work, and the routine and security required restrict the options available and turn the day into a different beast altogether (see Chapter 4). If he achieved masculinity through the dominance of others, these options become more dangerous inside the prison, where routes of escape from dangerous opponents are limited, and violence is seen to be an "acceptable" (albeit not institutionally) form of expression and retaliation.

---

women arguably internalise such pressures to a greater degree (seen in the pervasive nature of female self-harming within the prison estate [Borrill et al. 2005]), it is rare that their status as women will be called into question: it is the *quality* of their femaleness and feminine signifiers that can be called into question, rather than whether they 'count' as women at all. With men, however, their very status as a man is reliant upon their being able to prove their masculinities through such signifiers and performances, with the ultimate risk that, if they fail, they will be positioned out of masculinity and pushed into the realm of the feminine.

On top of these limitations to normative masculine signifiers, men in prison must attempt to sustain their masculinities in an environment where masculinities become competitive and, as a result, acknowledgement of the vulnerabilities they are experiencing as attacking their very being under-mines what masculinity they do have. Prisoners speak of the importance of maintaining a persona of strength and the ability to cope, in addition to the importance of 'doing your time'. The expressing of emotions and showing of weakness are not valorised, but instead demonstrate one's lack of ability to cope, a lack of manliness, and a potential target for exploita-tion. Where individuals fall into these categories, they acquire labels of vulnerability that are imposed by the institution which qualify them for special attention, differentiating them in negative ways from other prison-ers, and effectively positioning them outside the masculine hierarchy that prisoners value. Generally, these individuals are categorised according to a dichotomy of vulnerabilities, that being from others and from the self; yet this institutionalised dichotomy is situated far from notions of mas-culine identity, particularly when considering the importance of attaining individualism within the prison, and the problematic nature of applying categories of vulnerability to prisoners as institutional markers.

Individualism without Individuality, and the Vulnerability Dichotomy of Prisons

A key vulnerability emanates from the individual himself in terms of prisoners' vulnerable masculine identities. One of the key vulnerabili-ties of self that has been recognised in much academic investigation into the prisoner is that of individual identity—many prisoners tend to feel that they are reduced to a number or a commodity. Goffman's commentary on total institutions also discusses the notion of iden-tity and its adaptation within institutional settings, recognising that, as a result of a 'series of abasements, degradations, humiliations, and profanations of self [...] His self is systematically, if often uninten-tionally, mortified' (1961: 14), in addition to an individual undergo-ing changes in their 'moral career' (1961: 14). Similarly, Morris and Morris (1963) in their study of Pentonville prison in the late 1950s did discuss the concept of identity, particularly the loss of identity that prisoners underwent when joining such a large prison population—'many regard the submergence of their identity into the faceless mass as a major onslaught upon them as individuals' (1963: 167). As such, many prisoners tend to strive toward reinstating their individual identities, but this is problematic by virtue of the application of labels such as 'prisoner', and the sense of warehousing that occurs within a prison—each prisoner is another example of a man in a cell, often with similar needs, similar backgrounds, similar vulnerabilities, similar responses to their predicament, similar clothing, similar build etc. Although men differ according to race and age, the differences are often overwhelmed by the similar features. Additionally, reports of prisons and prisoners note the importance of individual identity with respect to masculinity:

Researcher:	You said that you don't feel like a man in prison, why, why is that?
Elliot:	Well it's coz like they're taking all your identity away and em...they take all your identity away from you, you're just a number in prison [...] Yeah. You're just a number in prison really

The problem prisoners are faced with, therefore, is the tension between achieving individualism without having individuality. By this, I mean that many prisoners strive to differentiate themselves from the prison majority (see Chapter 6)—yet they can never escape the fact that they are prisoners and will have that label tarnishing their identity for the rest of their lives. Even if they move away from a life of crime, their experiences of prison will undoubtedly shape their future identities; they can never escape from this identity label, which—by virtue of its stigma and connotations in society—erodes individuality. The man may well be able to differentiate himself from other prisoners through seeking education, through comparing his criminal actions, through his familial identity (all of which are different ways that he can display and prove his masculine sense of self in various ways that both comply and deviate from the hegemonic norms)—but he will never be able to differentiate himself from the prisoner label: because he will always have been a prisoner. Even those imprisoned and later acquitted of their crimes—although no longer labelled 'offenders'—will always have been prisoners. As Jefferson so adeptly notes, 'Release (from prison) is not equivalent to freedom' (2010: 403).

Where vulnerabilities are acknowledged within the prison, they tend to be seen in two ways—potential harms from others and potential harms from the self. Both of these themes are useful in terms of distinguishing those that the institution needs to invest particular resources in, in order to achieve security within the prison. Yet they are also highly problematic, not least in the ways in which they differentiate the labelled prisoners and give little thought to the implications such differentiation can have for individuals with regard to the masculine sense of self. The importance of differentiation as a tool used by prisoners runs throughout this book, but this form of imposed differentiation is different. Prisoners tend to want to achieve an individual masculine identity in the prison, which they must balance against the tensions resulting from a degradation of individual identity through institutionalisation; however, this must be achieved by the individual himself in order to be of any value to him as a person. Where he has differentiation imposed upon him, he actually undergoes even more of a "degradation" of individual self—he is placed into a category of 'other', which removes him from the prisoner collective who provide him with a masculine identity that he can impose his individualism against, the canvas upon which he can paint himself as a different kind of 'man'. At the same time, it places him into another grouping which he must differentiate himself from—the vulnerable—but also erodes his masculine credentials through the implication of weakness by virtue of being in such a group. As O'Donnell and Edgar note, 'Prisoners who are successfully isolated are confirmed in their vulnerability' (1998: 275).

With this in mind, the individual must attempt to differentiate himself from two groups—the prisoner collective and the vulnerable category—whilst also attempting to regain some form of masculine identity *and* negotiate the very vulnerabilities that placed him in the category in the first place. It is difficult to see what resources are available to an individual who is bullied, for example, who must (a) place himself as different from other prisoners as a whole, (b) place himself as different from other vulnerable prisoners, (c) demonstrate and prove himself to be masculine, and (d) negotiate being bullied and a target of exploitation, at the same time. The lack of engagement with notions of masculine self in processes of applying categorisations of vulnerability, other than the need to segregate, have the result that individuals become seen as 'other', not fulfilling masculine credentials, either by virtue of being dominated by others, or as a result of the internalisation of prison pains through self-harm. In a Canadian study (Ricciardelli et al. 2015), such vulnerabilities were seen dichotomised into physical and emotional. When intertwined, we can see some consistency with the ideas set forth here: at the heart of all such vulnerabilities are notions of visibility, audience, and control over performances of masculinities.

Vulnerability to Others

On the one hand vulnerability is seen through the lens of violence and physical and sexual harms from others (or the potential of such victimisation). Such vulnerability is quite real: the Ministry of Justice reports that, in the 12 months ending June 2015, 16,895 assault incidents occurred in male establishments in England and Wales (2015: 19). The interaction between masculinity and vulnerability is generally only viewed as negative or depreciated, rather than a non-presumptive consideration of how 'vulnerable' men perform (both positively and negatively) their own masculinities. Edgar et al. (2003) do discuss the concept of fear of crime, concepts of safety and personal harm avoidance, and then—more specifically—the Vulnerable Prisoner Unit context of avoidance of harm from others through segregation. This is, however, very much about the fear of others, and no consideration is given to more convoluted personal vulnerabilities with respect to masculinities and male identities. Some reference to machismo and status were considered by McCorkle (1992) with reference to which individuals opted for 'passive precaution' or 'aggressive precaution' factors to avoid personal victimisation (1992: 166). It was recognised that challenges to such signifiers of (masculine) reputation tended to trigger more severe moments of victimisation, but such avoidance of these elements through passivity, whilst reducing their personal risk of victimisation, were:

> generally interpreted by aggressive inmates as signs of weakness and vulnerability, those who employ them risk being assigned to a pool of victims who can easily be robbed or more generally exploited or dominated. (1992: 170)

There tends to be a presumption that the potential for aggressive precautionary measures is necessary for the avoidance of perceptions of vulnerability. Rather than being seen as different types of men, non-aggressive individuals are, arguably, seen as *lesser* men. Unfortunately, McCorkle does allude to the importance of certain negative behaviours in the creation of successful prison masculine identities, but does not then explain why that should be within the context of masculine behaviour, or explore further identity behaviours.

The notion of physical victimisation by others being *the* signifier of vulnerability is both restrictive and vague. Physical violence and victimisation may be one aspect that indicates an individual's vulnerabilities within the social context, but even that is problematic. As O'Donnell and Edgar argue, 'much victimization is mutual' (1999: 98), and whether an individual feels vulnerable as a result will be wholly subjective. Although many prisoners who were officially classified as vulnerable were subjected to violence or threats from others who judged their masculine performances, the concepts of vulnerability I encountered extended beyond the 'vulnerable' inmates and was much more concerned with personal vulnerabilities, including those that others may not see in everyday interactions.

Vulnerability from the Self

The second popular lens through which vulnerabilities are identified is centred on individual internalised vulnerabilities such as mental illness, emotional harm, and depression. Self-harm is a serious issue in prison, with the Ministry of Justice reporting that:

> the number of reported male self-harm incidents increased by 23 % in the 12 months to June 2015 to 21,702 incidents compared with 17,672 incidents in the 12 months to June 2014. This continues the long term trend of the number of self-harm incidents amongst male prisoners increasing. (2015: 16)

The gendered nature of self-focused vulnerability has been recognised, to a degree, in work with female prisoners. Borrill et al. note the high proportion of women self-harmers within the prison population, recognising associations between such behaviours and prior sexual abuse, bereavement, loss or rejection, mental health problems, familial concerns, bullying, and the prison experience itself (2005: 60–63). In practice, many such signifiers emerged in my interviews and 'most prisoners who kill themselves in custody are male, reflecting the larger male prison population' (Borrill et al. 2005: 57). Such a gendered difference in experiences and resultant behaviours merits more consideration in relation to the constituent of self and perceptions of (gendered) identity. Consideration of such issues has been given to recently released prisoners. One study found that 21 % of individuals who committed suicide within a year of release did so within 28 days, and 'men were eight times and women 36 times more likely to die by suicide within 1 year of release from prison than would be expected in their respective sex groups in the general population' (Pratt et al. 2006: 121). Liebling (with various colleagues) has performed a substantial body of work regarding the self-harming and suicidal behaviours of prisoners and recognises the vulnerabilities to suicide that exist within the prison population to be linked to demographic factors and psychiatric and personality disorders. Arguably these vulnerabilities are vulnerabilities of identity.

Although gendered differences in suicide are recognised—Liebling notes that 'it is unwise to make direct comparisons between the male and female prison populations as they are hardly equivalent' (2007: 443)—nonetheless, that is not a reason not to consider such differences as aspects of gender rather than the prison. Certainly the Samaritans note when discussing the fact that men in the UK are three times more likely than women to commit suicide (not in the prison context):

> Masculinity – the way men are brought up to behave and the roles, attributes and behaviours that society expects of them – contributes to suicide in men. Men compare themselves against a masculine 'gold standard' which prizes power, control and invincibility. When men believe they are not meeting this standard, they feel a sense of shame and defeat. Having a job and being able to provide for your family is central to 'being a man', particularly for working class men. Masculinity is associated with control, but when men are depressed or in crisis, they can feel out of control. This

can propel some men towards suicidal behaviour as a way of regaining control. (2012: 1)

Liebling notes that many of the aspects that are found to reduce distress within high-vulnerability groups are employment, personal development through offending behaviour courses, and family contact (2007: 436), elements that are inherently linked to components and signifiers of positive masculine identity performance.

As such, men in prison tend to be institutionally labelled according to these harms from others or the self, yet, as has been noted, the very label of vulnerability, when imposed on a prisoner, can have serious implications for how he is seen by others, and how he sees himself.

Experiences of Vulnerabilities

Whilst the label of vulnerability tends to have negative implications for individuals in terms of being associated with weakness and inferring problematic implications for masculine identity, many prisoners' testimonies demonstrated emotions and experiences that arguably fall within the realms of vulnerabilities—even if not labelled in that way by the individual himself. In this study, such experiences tended to fall into three distinct categories: vulnerabilities emanating from the outside world, vulnerabilities developed inside the prison, and vulnerabilities of the self.

Vulnerabilities: The Outside World

In interviews with prisoners, many accounts showed unspoken vulnerabilities that could be indirectly observed. Although participants spoke of particular groups of people as being vulnerable—those who accrued debt, certain offence types, those who had been bullied, older prisoners, first-time prisoners, the physically and mentally ill or disabled, those who could not speak English/read/write, and those who could not cope with prison—vulnerabilities experienced by all prisoners were evident. That said, many spoke of their inability to be vulnerable with others and the fact that showing one's self to be vulnerable was a sign of weakness, requiring negotiation to ensure security and reduce anxiety (see also Chapter 6):

Researcher: Can you talk to people in jail?
Bailey: Yeah, course you can. I mean I wouldn't talk to everybody like because…I don't know, some people still see that vulnerability and want to take advantage of that you know so…for me I talk to certain people, you'll have your little support group won't you so

As noted, vulnerabilities tended to be discussed relative to three categories—those related to the outside world; those related to their worlds within the prison; and vulnerabilities regarding the self and identities as individuals. With reference to the outside world, participants spoke about their families—their concerns about their relationships with partners and children (and, less often, friends) whilst they were in prison, and the importance of these relationships in getting prisoners through their sentences, as already discussed in Chapter 6. Numerous participants spoke of the problems they had in their relationships with their children, with some not being able to see them, others not wanting their children to come into prison, not being able to talk freely or frankly with them, or missing out on their lives whilst incarcerated. Participants spoke of the differences in behaviour that they displayed to their family in comparison to their prison associates (two very different audiences who both matter, but for very different reasons at very different times), and the manner in which this was restricted by other prisoners being present in the visiting area (see Crewe 2014).

Many spoke of the importance of visits and phone calls when they were having bad days (and the problems that they experienced with getting visits from people who lived far away), and how these could help when no one in prison could, due to the lack of trust felt between prisoners and the fact that prisoners had to appear emotionally hardened to each other. Participants were able to be more vulnerable and show more emotions in interactions with people outside the prison system, and spoke about this emotional incongruence. They also spoke of visitors exposing their emotional and vulnerable sides as a negative aspect, which sometimes resulted in them asking family members not to visit them in order to avoid such experiences and emotional reactions. Some felt that they had let their family down by being in prison, and spoke of feelings of failure on a wider scale:

Sebastian: No, I mean…the big majority of my family don't even know I'm in prison […] Coz like, you know there's no one in my family that's ever been to prison so you know my Mum and all that, she doesn't really, I've told her you know if you want to tell the family tell them but…she, I know she don't so, but she won't, she won't lie she won't say, if they say where's [prisoner], she'll say he's in [Town name] But she just won't say it's in prison […]

Such feelings demonstrate emotional vulnerability and the impacts that imprisonment can have upon men's self-confidence and views of themselves, particularly as male figures through the eyes of those who matter to them (or at least, how they think they might be perceived). These perceptions are also influenced by the past lives of the participants—the involvement of the care system in the lives of many prisoners has been discussed in Chapter 4—and, in addition to this, the vulnerability of individuals was evident in their discussions of experiences of abuse, a lack of educational achievement, and their criminal and problematic pasts, particularly with reference to drink and drug addictions on the outside, highlighting periods of their lives where they lacked control. Participants also spoke of their feelings of insecurity regarding their future post-prison lives, whether they would be able to stay crime free and thus achieve masculinity legitimately by attaining employment and housing, staying away from substance temptations, or achieving their hopes and aspirations for the future (see also Chapter 4), showing a level of vulnerability of the self with reference to their hopes and fears, their 'potential masculinities', and the wish to stay away from prison.

Vulnerabilities: The World within the Prison

Participants highlighted numerous vulnerabilities in their lives within the prison. Physically, participants spoke of their feelings of threat and insecurity, and the fact that they had observed (and sometimes experienced or undertaken) violence, bullying, and confrontations within the prison, which had often influenced their following behaviours. The theme of the body has been discussed already in Chapter 3, and highlights certain personal vulnerabilities when participants felt the need to show strength through their bodies and physical abilities in the gym. In addition, the theme of health highlights the vulnerabilities participants experienced in respect to their futures and the temporary nature of their life courses. A number of participants also spoke of the drastic measures that they had taken (against property and people) in order to attain a level of security within the prison following threats of harm from others, with some reaching a level of physical vulnerability that required their segregation. Participants spoke of places and spaces where they felt particularly vulnerable to harm from others, with locations where staff were less visible recognised as being of risk. At the same time, some spoke of the ways in which they felt vulnerable at the hands of staff, having allegedly observed or experienced abuse or breaches of trust in past prisons, and due to the fact that staff had a high degree of control over them:

William: Well they've got so much control, haven't they over, over your life when you go to the toilet, when you eat, who you speak to, when you speak to them, it's your whole, they invade your whole being

Such a sense of invasion is particularly punitive as it strikes at the heart of male autonomy, independence, and control over the self—highly masculine attributes that are central to adult hegemonic masculinity. Many highlighted the vulnerabilities that they had felt within young offenders' institutions in the past, due to perceiving that they had something to prove. It appears that young offenders' institutions in particular engendered both physical vulnerabilities and vulnerabilities of identity and the self. Such feelings of vulnerability to harm from others appear to be directly connected to an individual's lack of control over the actions and interpretations of others—similar to Jackson's notion of 'laddishness' as a self-protection strategy (2002)—showing disempowerment and revealing the extent to which being in control is a key aspect of masculine identity. Attempts to escape or confront such vulnerabilities, therefore, actually exemplify this.

In the context of the adult prison, participants discussed the fact that there was violence and the presence of gang cultures, particularly on the 'main jail', in addition to there being a problem with drugs that promoted temptations to those trying to change their behaviours. Many spoke of the need to retain a sense of focus and self-control (with reference to such temptations and their reactions to others), and this was particularly visible with prisoners on indeterminate sentences who had to prove themselves to the authority audience for sentence progression, with many recognising the vulnerability of their status in relation to release. Such vulnerabilities of status were exacerbated by the fact that prisoners often had to wait for their paperwork to be completed, and delays had implications for their hearings, thus subjecting them to periods of high stress and uncertainty:

Freddie: Do you know what I mean, it's a very big part I mean I'm anxious about it now, and the thing is what people don't realise, other people, is that year for a lifer, that period of a year, your reports start, they, they start six months before, they're bound to be late because of what's going on so you've got a year of just pure stress, it's just pure stress, I'm under pure stress now and I really, that's why I'd rather melt down and flake and not have to try to deal with people that I don't have to deal with coz I've got a lot of other things to deal with

Uncertainties made participants feel vulnerable due to their lack of direct control over certain aspects of their lives, such as their sentences, the actions of others, their lives on the outside, and so on, with the eventual consequence of individuals becoming institutionalised and dependent upon others (and thereby achieving certainty at the expense of control and autonomy—see also Ricciardelli et al. 2015). This was particularly poignant as many acknowledged the importance of maintaining some form of independence and self-sufficiency in order to feel positive about themselves. Again, this suggests these values to be deeply culturally associated with 'successful' masculinity and hegemonic ideals (Connell 2005).

To try to achieve this, prisoners performed aspects of identity and took on different personalities in order to avoid exposing personal vulnerabilities, such as emotions and feelings, which could be perceived as weaknesses in the hypermasculine culture of the prison, and thus be taken advantage of:

Kai: The reason that I have to put a front on every day is so, is letting other prisoners know that I'm not a certain way myself [...] You know so they in actual fact are forcing me to do that, coz if I were to be myself then people would think oh you're weak or you're vulnerable to this or...can we, can we get round him that way d'you know what I mean

Many noted to me how things that they observed *were* scary and how they did feel afraid in some instances, and many spoke of the fact that they could not be themselves in prison. The need to maintain a level of emotional toughness and the subsequent lack of trust has already been recognised in Chapter 6, yet numerous participants spoke of the benefits that they had experienced in being able to drop this, to a degree, and their ability to accept vulnerability and to speak on a more open and emotional level. This was particularly the case when undertaking group work or when in therapeutic environments, where prisoners formed communities of support and openness in order to engage with and address offending behaviours:

Ethan: [...] a lot of that I've learned from, from therapy because like, every morning you're there to talk about, someone gets to use the group and they get to talk about their issues so you kind of get to know people and, and like there's people coming up first and you'll see what they're like at first and then, and then you kind of just...oh, like it's really interesting to just watch them develop and, and try and see what their faults are, d'you know what I mean, you kind of see when they're kind of just having a bravado and all this and that, but then you can also see people when they break down and just start crying and that and, and that can be, um, yeah it's emotional but at the same time it's really good because...um, that's what people are always hiding in jail, they're always hiding their emotions and stuff like that, I've done it, and you know that's probably why I've been in and out of jail all my life

Such 'hiding' points to the importance of the maintenance of a masculine front of emotional toughness for the benefit of the hypermasculine gaze both of other prisoners and of staff members (see Chapter 3). It is also for the benefit of the individual himself in terms of the type of man he sees himself, and wishes to be seen as (generally as someone who can sustain his independence and self-control), which he too will judge relative to the masculine culture that he is immersed in and which is perpetually at risk of being policed in various harmful and emasculating manners.

Vulnerabilities: The Self

Participants spoke of their personal vulnerabilities that emerged when they were alone in their cells (for long periods, generally at night), and the fact that they felt the need to keep busy or distracted in order to avoid thinking too much about their personal situations (and emotional feelings of failure or separation from the outside world), which had the potential to result in negative emotions and potential actions. On a number of occasions, the exaggerative effects of prison upon 'problems' were mentioned:

Jude: Everything's intensified you know it's like being in a...pressure cooker, you know, everything, you know, a little problem outside that you wouldn't think twice about in here is a major issue

Negative emotions and experiences of the prison were widely experienced, although the importance of being supported through one's sentence, the value of positive interactions (numerous participants spoke of how they helped and advised other prisoners, or had been helped and advised themselves), and the need to get along with other prisoners, was acknowledged. Many also noted the fact that there was a general lack of trust in prison, that prison 'friendships' were generally temporary in nature (see Chapter 6), and the need to police one's words and actions in order to avoid trouble with others. As such, the masculine solidarity that existed in prisons of old appears to have been eroded, although there was acknowledgement of the fact that:

William: You know we're all in the same boat, and if we don't have a little bit of respect for those around us then it's all just going to go to pot I think

Prisoners have to sustain a level of individualism, yet not generally be individuals due to their status as numbered prisoners, which impacts upon how they are treated and creates a sense of vulnerability with respect to their personal identities as independent, individual men. Other self-destructive tendencies were mentioned as due to, and contributing to, a climate of isolation and alienation, despite the size of the prison population. Participants spoke of their vulnerabilities at the hands of others, with a number highlighting the effect that certain prisoners could have upon their mental well-being through their own negativity (and vice versa with positive people) and the impacts of peer pressure. Others were often seen as having actual negative effects—participants spoke of the discomfort that other prisoners produced in them due to their offences, personal hygiene, and mere presence with the accompanying lack of privacy, highlighting the fact that individuals can feel vulnerable due to their inability to predict or control others:

Sebastian: Because it's mixed in you don't know who you're talking to do you […] And that's not, that's not nice […] coz I've got pictures like pictures like my step kids, my nieces, my nephews all over the walls and I think to myself, hold on a minute this geezer's walking into my cell, he's looking round my cell, "oh these are nice pictures", I'm thinking, I'm thinking some nasty things, I'm thinking why are you looking at my pictures, are you looking at my pictures coz they're nice or are you looking at them coz you're a wrong un[2]

Participants tended to show traits that could be seen as vulnerabilities with reference to losing control over some aspect(s) of their lives in the harsh environment of the prison—at least one participant described feeling 'trapped', highlighting the lack of control he experienced and perceived. With many there were obvious underlying issues from their pasts that had impacted upon their criminal futures and their masculine identities and abilities (such as their abilities as fathers). It was clear that many participants could be classed as vulnerable or victims before they became entangled in the criminal justice system, with implications for their self-esteem and confidence. When these issues were identified and engaged with in 'safe' environments where individuals generally took a much less judgmental stance towards each other's displays of emotion and "weakness" participants often felt more able to show a degree of emotionality and vulnerability to others, where they would not as standard due to the negative implications of being seen as weak. In order to retain a level of control over themselves, participants spoke of the fact that they put up fronts to other prisoners to hide their true identities with their associated emotions and weaknesses. This was seen to have implications for how generous or kind individuals could be to each other, with trust being at a premium:

---

[2] Referring to sex offenders.

Connor: You know…not a lot of them are like that in here though, […] they say
           there's no one like you, you know, you, you're the only person that actually
           cares, and I do and it's a downfall really, in here, because…to care in a place
           like this, you're either soft, gay, or hiding something

Ownership

Throughout the book, I have repeated the importance of ownership to
individuals in terms of their masculinities: the ownership of time, the
ownership of possessions, the ownership of spaces (see also Sloan
2012a, b). Ownership is also salient in the sphere of vulnerabilities in
prison and speaks to the heart of vulnerable masculinities. In prison,
there is often no means through which men are able to take ownership
of their own vulnerabilities in conformity with their masculine identity.
When vulnerable to harm from others, individuals are made vulnerable
by virtue of how others respond to them—vulnerability is forced upon
them by the watching audience. When labelled as vulnerable by the institution, although they may accept this label, it has been applied to them:
it is ultimately the institutional audience's, not the individual's. Where
individuals are vulnerable to harm from themselves, it is arguable that they
do take ownership of their vulnerabilities—they impose control over it by
internalising the pain and inflicting it upon themselves. Yet this is seen in
terms of femininity—it fails to conform to the masculine conceptions of
violence being something to use upon others. One prisoner actually noted
this when talking about others' responses to his own self-harming:

Noah: […] I said because to me it's like coping at times. Ok it's not normal to
          you…I said but you, I said you'd consider me going along and hitting
          someone else normal behaviour, whereas cutting, hurting myself, that's not
          normal […]

In the 'normal' prison estate,[3] there is no legitimate sphere were men are
able to engage directly with their vulnerabilities, free from risks of erosion

---

[3] Although one prisoner did highlight the ability to do such identity work and emotional engagement within specified therapeutic environments, yet these are often restrictive in terms of who can
engage with them with reference to sentence types, lengths, and the prisoners themselves.

of their masculine identities (although the organisation *Safe Ground* does attempt to do this in the prisons that it works within). If prisoners talk to other prisoners, they are seen to be unable to cope or lacking in qualities of toughness or resilience, whereas if they engage with the institutional gateways for vulnerability their masculinities risk become damaged further and subject to stigmatising labels. In an environment where ownership of the self is seen to be of high value, and being able to maintain a masculine façade of toughness and emotional resilience is extremely significant, there are few means for prisoners to achieve any form of emotional support in order to deal with their ontological insecurities and masculine vulnerabilities. Few courses in prison are available to help men be better men, and those that do exist are certainly not the norm, nor are they available to everyone. In addition, the sources of support that men might otherwise turn to, such as their families and friends, are also subject to scrutiny (not least from their family and friends)—men are watched by other men in visiting areas (see also Crewe et al. 2014); men are listened to by other men when on the phone with a queue of other users behind them; and even if men get the opportunity to have time to themselves in their cells, they are ultimately, on their own:

Samuel: So when I came to jail, all these things I hid behind was just totally, psss, taken away…and all I was left with was a steel door…um…I think that's why I went into depression, because all of a sudden I was alone, I was vulnerable…I didn't know what to do I was in no control of my life whatsoever, because I think that's also part of why, um…I did certain things, to kind of gain that sense of control in my life, and…all that was taken away from me, like I said, when I came to jail, and it was just left with me…and I fell into depression, and…there was nothing to hide behind

In a situation where men have already proven their inability to do masculinity legitimately, where they often lack the emotional resources to deal with their problems in socially constructive manners, and where they are constantly under the masculine microscope from audiences that matter to them, such masculine vulnerabilities can ultimately result in the changing of the individual and how he 'deals' with his vulnerabilities. It is arguable that the high rates of violence and harm that are experienced within the prison are actually ways through which individuals can reframe their expressions of vulnerability—rather than engaging with and discussing the vulnerabilities being felt as impinging upon an individual's masculinity, men shift the discursive means. As Liebling and Krarup note:

> Those most vulnerable (the 'feminine' group in Jack's theory of attempted suicide in women) are exposed to failure in a highly 'masculine' environment, where – to use his analogy, only the 'macho' survive. Imprisonment for men may actually demand the worst excesses of 'masculinity', in their least legitimate form, from those who find a way of coping successfully with it. It is less surprising, in this theoretical context, that 'the weak' and 'the inadequate' are so labelled, and require 'protection'. (1993: 162)

Violence and harm are forms of communication, but the message is often lost in the physical and mental harms that are experienced by the victim. Crawley and Crawley note that violence within prisons can take on three functions—instrumentality, expression, and communication through performance—whereby violence 'can transmit meaning to an audience far wider than its intended recipient' (2008: 126). The role of violence in prisons as a manner through which to communicate or perform masculine identities has been recognised on numerous occasions (Sim 1994; Thurston 1996), though the links between masculinity and vulnerability are rarely equally considered, continuing the stereotypical association of violence with male power. If we bring masculine vulnerabilities into the equation, perhaps it is more useful to see this association with power as being more about a lack of discursive power in that, ultimately, men cannot and do not talk about their vulnerabilities and problems, but often create more masculinely acceptable problems in order to prove their masculine credentials. The harms imposed upon others are symptomatic of the lack of ability to express the vulnerabilities men experience to their masculine identities by virtue of being in prison and having their legitimate masculinities, and all opportunities to retain them, gradually whittled away.

What about those who do not resort to violence? Simply because an individual does not partake in the violence, dominance, or other harmful or socially illegitimate behaviours does not necessarily mean that they are not engaging with the process. Brownmiller made the same point with reference to rape: 'It is nothing more or less than a conscious process of intimidation by which *all* men keep *all* women in a state of fear' (1975: 15). In the same way, although not all men in prison commit harmful behaviours, they rarely openly condemn such actions, and will themselves benefit from the hierarchical structure that does not automatically position them at the bottom. Although men who are vulnerable may not choose harmful means through which to express such gendered vulnerabilities, they are not challenging the system and openly engaging with or expressing their own masculine vulnerabilities in other ways (opting instead for no open engagement), and they are not openly criticising the discursive means chosen by others. In the same way that all men benefit from rape, in prison, all men benefit from the harmful communicative means chosen to demonstrate masculine vulnerabilities by virtue of the fact that those that do commit violence retain a system whereby direct emotional engagement (the "difficult" option) is policed and prevented or institutionalised. The problem is, in this instance, those that benefit are also those that suffer, in that the masculine vulnerabilities still go unheard and unresolved.

Reflexive Note

Whilst in prison, men's masculine vulnerabilities and my own gendered identity intersected in ways which were illuminative of the gendered vulnerabilities being experienced by men, particularly regarding the lack of female identities against which they were able to juxtapose their masculinities. Many such vulnerabilities have already been discussed in the reflexive notes of preceding chapters. I was very lucky in that I rarely felt overly vulnerable within the prison—although my identity management was a personal challenge, and I was restricted in my movements and temporal experiences; and although I was also watched throughout the day, my vulnerabilities were nowhere near as problematic as those of many men in prison, nor of the staff. For example, one day I came into the prison to find out that one of the staff members I was chatting with had had to cut down someone who had attempted to hang himself the day before. The implications of such experiences for the suicidal man, and for the staff member having to take action, are feelings that take notions of vulnerability to a whole new level. The fact that staff members carry ligature knives with them as a matter of course, and yet prisoners cannot use metal cutlery (but can use razor blades) really does challenge one's thinking of prisons and their priorities.

One of the central tenets of vulnerability is the notion of being, in some way, at risk. I rarely felt that within the prison, mainly because I was normally in some degree of control over my movements, use of time, personal identity, and when I wanted to leave. These were all dimensions that were categorically denied to the men that I was interviewing. Having experienced some of the gendered vulnerabilities that emerged in the prison setting as an observer—and therefore to a degree nowhere near as intense or inescapable as those actually living (and working) in prisons—it becomes clear that gender, vulnerabilities, and imprisonment are tightly connected and have serious implications for each other and the men experiencing them.

Summary

Vulnerabilities and masculinities are two subjects that are rarely engaged with in academic and policy discourse, particularly not together. Yet physical and mental vulnerabilities are often the result of sustained immersion in a hypermasculine setting such as the prison, and can themselves have implications for the masculinities of the individual and others who situate their genders relative to him. This chapter brings a new dimension to discourse regarding male vulnerabilities. Although recognition has been made of the associations between masculine identities and vulnerabilities with regard to how individuals behave for distinct audiences with the available gendered resources (see Kimmel 1994; Wolf-Light 1994), and although the physical and mental vulnerabilities associated within processes of imprisonment are also regularly considered, rarely are these two notions drawn together. This chapter has shown how vulnerability in prison is intrinsically linked to masculine identity—rather than simply seeing vulnerability in terms of physical or mental harms, potential harms to gendered identity are seen to result from imprisonment due, in part, to a lack of control or certainty over the self (see also Ricciardelli et al. 2015 for synergy with the Canadian experience). Although this could have been anticipated with regard to those individuals who become labelled as weak and vulnerable through their location on the wing for vulnerable prisoners, this chapter has actually shown that vulnerabilities in men are much more extensively experienced.

The vulnerabilities experienced tend to manifest into three spheres—the outside world, the internal world of the prison, and the internalised world of the self and personal identity. In addition, vulnerabilities shape and are shaped by the three realms of the past, present, and future, generally centred around notions of disempowerment and a lack of control over some sphere or time of one's life. Other men have substantial impacts upon an individual man's vulnerabilities, with many having to hide their vulnerabilities from others in order to disguise weaknesses and appear emotionally tough to gain masculine credentials (Kimmel 1994), often simply reformulating their vulnerabilities into communications that are viewed in a more masculine fashion, such as violence and harm to others.

Vulnerabilities and masculinities are inherently linked, shaping the ways men feel that they can or should be men, be that through the processes of putting on a front to try to hide one's vulnerable self, through the performance of emotionally tough personas, through distancing oneself from negative labels of weakness, or through limiting the degree of trust or friendship shown towards others in the reduction and management of risks to masculine identity.

References

Borrill, J., Snow, L., Medlicott, D., Teers, R., & Paton, J. (2005). Learning from 'Near Misses': Interviews with women who survived an incident of severe self-harm in prison. *The Howard Journal, 44*(1), 57–69.

Brownmiller, S. (1975). *Against our will: Men, women and rape.* London: Penguin. New York: Fawcett Books.

Connell, R. W. (2005). *Masculinities* (2nd ed.). Cambridge: Polity Press.

Crawley, E., & Crawley, P. (2008). Culture, performance, and disorder: The communicative quality of prison violence. In J. M. Byrne, D. Hummer, & F. S. Taxman (Eds.), *The culture of prison violence.* Boston: Pearson/Allyn and Bacon.

Crewe, B. (2014). Not looking hard enough masculinity, emotion, and prison research. *Qualitative Inquiry, 20*(4), 392–403.

Crewe, B., Warr, J., Bennett, P., & Smith, A. (2014). The emotional geography of prison life. *Theoretical Criminology, 18*(1), 56–74.

Edgar, K., O'Donnell, I., & Martin, C. (2003). *Prison violence: The dynamics of conflict, fear and power.* Cullompton: Willan Publishing.

Giddens, A. (1991). *Modernity and self-identity: Self and society in the late modern age.* Cambridge: Polity Press.

Goffman, E. (1961). *Asylums: Essays on the social situation of mental patients and other inmates.* Chicago: Aldine Publishing Company.

Jackson, C. (2002). 'Laddishness' as a self-worth protection strategy. *Gender and Education, 14*(1), 37–50.

Jefferson, A. M. (2010). Traversing sites of confinement post-prison survival in Sierra Leone. *Theoretical Criminology, 14*(4), 387–406.

Kimmel, M. S. (1994). Masculinity as homophobia: Fear, shame, and silence in the construction of gender identity. In H. Brod & M. Kaufman (Eds.), *Theorizing masculinities.* Thousand Oaks and London: Sage.

Laing, R. D. (1960). *The divided self: An existential study in sanity and madness.* Harmondsworth: Penguin.

Liebling, A. (2007). Prison suicide and its prevention. In Y. Jewkes (Ed.), *Handbook on prisons.* Cullompton: Willan Publishing.

Liebling, A., & Krarup, H. (1993). *Suicide attempts and self-injury in male prisons.* London: Home Office Research and Planning Unit for the Prison Service.

McCorkle, R. C. (1992). Personal precautions to violence in prison. *Criminal Justice and Behaviour, 19*(2), 160–173.

Ministry of Justice. (2015). *Safety in custody statistics England and Wales deaths in prison custody to September 2015 assaults and self-harm to June 2015,* Ministry of Justice Statistics Bulletin. Retrieved November, 2015 from https://www.gov.uk/government/uploads/system/uploads/attachment_data/file/472449/safety-in-custody.pdf

Morris, T., & Morris, P. (1963). *Pentonville: A sociological study of an English Prison.* London: Routledge and Kegan Paul.

O'Donnell, I., & Edgar, K. (1998). Routine victimisation in prisons. *The Howard Journal, 37*(3), 266–279.

O'Donnell, I., & Edgar, K. (1999). Fear in prison. *The Prison Journal, 79*(1), 90–99.

Pratt, D., Piper, M., Appleby, L., Webb, R., & Shaw, J. (2006). Suicide in recently released prisoners: A population-based cohort study. *The Lancet, 368,* 119–123.

Ricciardelli, R., Maier, K., & Hannah-Moffat, K. (2015). Strategic masculinities: Vulnerabilities, risk and the production of prison masculinities. *Theoretical Criminology, 19*(4), 491–513.

Samaritans. (2012). *Men, suicide and society: Why disadvantaged men in mid-life die by suicide.* Surrey: Samaritans. Retrieved November, 2015 from http://www.samaritans.org/sites/default/files/kcfinder/files/press/Men%20Suicide%20and%20Society%20Research%20Report%20151112.pdf

Sim, J. (1994). Tougher than the rest? Men in prison. In T. Newburn & E. A. Stanko (Eds.), *Just boys doing business? Men, masculinities and crime.* London and New York: Routledge.

Sloan, J. (2012a). 'You Can See Your Face in My Floor': Examining the function of cleanliness in an adult male prison. *The Howard Journal of Criminal Justice, 51*(4), 400–410.

Sloan, J. (2012b). Cleanliness, spaces and masculine identity in an adult male prison. *Prison Service Journal, 201*, 3–6.

Thurston, R. (1996). Are you sitting comfortably? Men's storytelling, masculinities, prison culture and violence. In M. Mac an Ghaill (Ed.), *Understanding masculinities: Social relations and cultural arenas.* Buckingham, UK: Open University Press.

Wolf-Light, P. (1994). The everyman centre. In A. Coote (Ed.), *Families, children and crime.* London: Institute for Public Policy Research.

8

Gender in Prison

Masculinity is, arguably, the central tenet underpinning and shaping the adult male prison experience. Masculinity can be seen woven into nearly every account in some manner, through the notions of control, ownership, dominance, or independence. During interviews, and when observing men in the general prison population, it was clear that masculinity played a key role. When staff shouted on the wings, or prisoners shouted between cells, they generally did so in a booming (almost animalistic) masculine tone, and numerous participants would describe examples of masculine presence in terms of deep vocal ranges and the flexing of muscles. They also did this to demonstrate masculine discourse for my benefit, in addition to using flirtatious comments, jokes, and innuendo.

In narratives too, participants described concepts that linked directly to masculine identity. The concept of performance was spoken of in terms of the demonstration of a physically and emotionally hard front in order to cover any sense of weakness for the masculine audience of the prison setting. The masculine audience plays a substantial role in the influencing of gendered behaviours within the prison. In addition to performing in stereotypically masculine arenas such as the gym and through symbolic markers such as sports, and objectifying women in discourse and displays

© The Editor(s) (if applicable) and The Author(s) 2016
J.A. Sloan, *Masculinities and the Adult Male Prison Experience*,
DOI 10.1057/978-1-137-39915-1_8

on cell walls (not all of them, it should be added), day-to-day activities and interactions were often governed by similar influences. Men spoke of the fact that they had to exert the potential to be violent and stand up for themselves if challenged, again in order to prevent the appearance of weakness. As such, violence was recognised be a risk, with many experiencing or witnessing real violence at some point in their prison careers. The protection of reputation and tough masculine image was seen to be particularly significant in this way and related on some occasions to an individual's reputation in the community:

Kevin: You have to make sure who's around as well because people think, even if that guy's not there, people think they can take the piss as well and like carry on [...] D'you know what I mean. In prison it's all about reputation and stuff like that and you know what I mean, how big you are, if, if you're massive and

Researcher: You mean like physically?

Kevin: Physically big or you got a good reputation from wherever you come from

Reputation and proving oneself was seen to be a particularly prevalent occurrence within the young offender sphere of the prison estate, whereas the adult male estate was often described as being 'man's jail', where overt incidences of discord were discouraged (although an 'alpha male' hierarchy was still recognised by a few participants). Respect was seen to be of value by some, although others felt that this was irrelevant, a view that was somewhat undermined by the fact that individuals would police their identity for the benefit of other prisoners to gain some positive standing, which some might equate to respect. There was a sense of masculine competition, closely tied in with reputation and image, particularly in the field of hardness and personal wealth:

Sebastian: Mainly people talk about...how many girls they've had and how much money they've got and what they're going to do when they get out and my boys are this that and the other and just...nonsense really, d'you know what I mean

The two themes of hardness and wealth are indicators of hegemonic masculinity in other settings too (Connell 2005; Connell and Messerschmidt 2005). In terms of wealth, participants often spoke of the importance of being financially independent and working, tying in to the role of men as providers. In addition, this theme was used to demonstrate an individual's independence and self-sufficiency more broadly, which was generally lacking within the prison context:

Connor: So it was a case of right, I've got to do it myself, if they're not going to help me do it, I've got to do it myself, coz that's what I'm like outside, if, I won't ask anyone for nothing, if I need something I'll work and earn the money to go and get it, you know, very self-sufficient, d'you know what I mean, so in here I've just had to apply that and it's paid off

Men's roles within the family sphere were also esteemed, in spite of their removal from such institutions through imprisonment. Prison was seen to have a direct impact upon their abilities to be fathers in particular, as many felt that they did not want their children to visit, or that they could not fulfil their paternal roles adequately whilst inside. Some spoke of wanting more children—these men's fertility was clearly of importance to them, highlighting the importance of the healthy body to men's perceptions of themselves in present and future spheres, and patriarchal roles and the heterosexual family as highly regarded constituents of gendered identity. Family was often central to the framing of participants' current masculinities and their aspirations for future identities—they generally wanted to create or return to the 'normal' family setting, albeit some seeing the importance of taking some time to re-establish a settled life outside before doing so.

Such adherence to institutional norms and behavioural expectations were clear in the lives of many men, particularly with respect to the fronts that they had to put up for others. Many spoke of the fact that prison had changed them, particularly in terms of making them more mature:

Connor: I don't want to sound cheesy when I say it but it's like coming in a caterpillar and leaving a butterfly, d'you know what I mean? It's making that transformation from boy to man I suppose

Others spoke of the need for displays of strength, machismo, testosterone, and bravado that they experienced or observed within the prison sphere. In addition, participants spoke of the importance of maintaining a positive masculine identity in order to retain a sense of self-confidence, positive ego, and personal pride:

Researcher: D'you think it's a bad thing to be seen as vulnerable here?
Benjamin: Possibly yeah, especially if you're in a local jail… […] …and you've
               got friends that you know realise oh he was on the numbers[1] it's not a
               good thing […] Plus it's not good for your self, your self-respect […]
               I mean because obviously when I get out I wanna get, I wanna have
               a relationship with a woman and all that and it's…it's gonna be bad
               enough saying I've been in prison, if somebody says ah yeah he was
               on the Vulnerable Prisoners' Unit it's not good for the old uh ego

Prison, therefore, was seen to require a particular form of masculine identity in order for prisoners to be accepted, or not victimised or seen as vulnerable. Thought-provokingly, when asked directly about feelings regarding their manhood, the vast majority of participants from all locations stated that they did not feel more like a man in prison. Such distinct opinions regarding a lack of feelings of manliness within the prison are compelling when contextualised with the narratives emerging from interviews—although many men did not feel manly, they seemed to make serious concerted efforts towards achieving the appearance of manliness in front of others. The two notions may have been linked—because individuals did not feel more like men in prison, they may have felt the need to compensate for this through masculine efforts and performances, in spite of the hypermasculine setting, and the distinct masculine requirements and lack of female juxtapositioning. Perhaps this was the point—without women to position one's gender against (Connell 2005: 43), individuals' feelings of manhood were less able to contrast against femininity, and there was always the risk of men themselves being juxtaposed against each other, thus undermining their own masculinities, especially when subjected to feminised dimensions of corporeality, time, space, and gaze. As Irwin notes:

In the absence of females, however, with no opportunity to measure one's masculine appeal, and where all claims about past accomplishments are suspect and one has aged and fallen out of step, uncertainty about one's appeal to the opposite sex is likely to grow. (1970: 92)

---

[1] Referring to the Vulnerable Prisoners' Unit.

Maintaining control (over themselves, their personal space, their routines, or even others) was often described as being an influential factor in participants' daily lives. This was also linked to responsibilities—many participants recognised the fact that they had to take responsibility in their lives in some way, be that for their personal health and well-being by going to the gym or buying extra food, by managing their inner selves through putting on a front or taking time to relax (or finding ways to 'escape' or forget the prison), or by taking responsibility for their sentence progression and personal development. In this context, taking responsibility is closely tied with taking control over one's self, and is arguably of importance for participants in terms of their current identities (and personal well-being) and their potential future selves, not least because taking responsibility for one's self will enable an individual to be seen to be addressing his risk levels. Despite this, such efforts do not appear to have made individuals feel this was masculine, as if reflection and introspection are not manly processes—they were certainly recognised as not being as easy in the rush of daily life on the outside.

Masculinities, or male-centred behaviours and norms, pervade every aspect of participants' lives, from day-to-day activities, to future plans, to their perceptions, well-being, and personal security, and to their inner and outer selves. It is curious to observe that there are distinct forms of masculine norms within the prison that do not necessarily correspond to those norms in the outside world. Men are expected to survive within the prison though hiding emotions, displaying the potential for aggression, and taking control—within the prison, a front-line masculine identity must be externalised. Outside prison, such hypermasculine traits are increasingly being seen in a negative light—emotions are seen to be valuable for positive relationships and families; displays of aggression are criminalised or seen to be anti-social and dangerous; and overtly controlling others is seen in a negative light if done to too great a degree, though often defended by the violent individual as being the victim's fault, such as in instances of domestic violence and rape (see Koss et al. 1994). Extreme masculinity outside prison is much more acceptable when performed in institutionally acceptable ways such as the business or sports worlds—these are institutions of legitimate masculinity, unlike the institution of the prison. When considered in this way, we can see that prison masculine expectations are often incompatible with societal norms and requirements for successful legitimate masculinity, leading to some discord as men perform their masculinities through their own bodies and domestic roles, rather than through familial and institutional roles, albeit all such roles placing dimensions of control centre-stage.

Control

> ... *masculinity has as its intention the control of self and 'other'.* (Odih 1999: 19)

Control was an element that ran throughout the themes that emerged from the fieldwork, and was a concept that often highlighted the gendered natures of behaviours and interactions within the prison. Control differs from responsibility, which is defined as being where someone is:

> liable to be called to account as being in charge or control; answerable (to a person, etc. *for* something); deserving the blame or credit of (with *for*); governed by a sense of responsibility; being a free moral agent; morally accountable for one's actions. (The Chambers Dictionary 2003: 1290)

In this context in that such use of control is not enforceable by others—although failure to achieve masculinity can result in demarcation and derision from the masculine prison collective—no one can say that actions that assert ownership over people, spaces, or selves have particular 'moral accountability'. Similarly, control does not necessarily equate to 'power': 'the skill, physical ability, opportunity or authority to do something; strength or energy; force or effectiveness' (The Chambers Dictionary 2003: 1182).

The majority of men in prison are, by their very situation, disempowered and lack a degree of legitimate masculine authority. Power is sometimes taken too far in discussions of gender—Kaufman states that 'the common feature of the dominant forms of contemporary masculinity is that manhood is equated with having some sort of power' (1994: 145). Arguably, however, this is too simplistic a determination. Men in prison can have masculine status whilst being socially disempowered. In addition, if one considers control on a broader level, not simply forms of interpersonal domination as Kaufman discusses (1994: 146) instead of power, a new dimension is added to the situation. Power tends to be situated in terms of interpersonal relations and is arguably conferred through the eyes and responses of others (the performance for an audience), whereas control is much more about influences that individuals acquire and exert over others and their selves and spaces (performance for the self). These two dimensions of performance need to sit together to be successful achievements of masculinity. Power is a salient matter in prisoners' lives, and personal empowerment can be associated with control of the self. Throughout prisoners' accounts, men spoke in terms that implied the importance of three distinct elements of control: the control of others, the control of personal space, and the control of self.

The Control of Others

Individuals spoke of the way that they controlled their associations and audiences both in prison and outside. Outside the prison, there was often reference to the hierarchical ranking of potential visitors and support networks—family ranked highest relative to friends, for example. In addition, associations that allowed a degree of control over the individual's life course were highly valued (such as legal teams and sentences, or partners and the individual's familial role). Some prisoners also spoke of the testing of associations outside, where friendships were put on hold in order to gauge their reliability, thus allowing an individual to control his surrounding support network. Such control over outside relationships and interactions allowed individuals to exert some degree of control over their gendered identity performances. Familial or partner ties allowed men to perform masculine roles through the expression of sexual and emotional identity signifiers—emotionality was seen to be acceptable in certain instances in the context of the family. Men could juxtapose their masculinities against the women in their lives (if only somewhat symbolically), in a manner that was generally unavailable to them within the prison setting.

Inside the prison, men controlled the very nature of interactions on a physical and symbolic level through the differentiation of exchanges according to the varying labels applied (see also Chapter 6). The recognition of such interactions as situational, transient, and temporary allowed individuals to demonstrate control over them—their very lack of permanence acted as an indicator of the choice to interact and thus the control an individual had over who he decided to spend time with and perform for. Individuals controlled such associations through gendered performances, which allowed interactions to take on distinctive natures—men controlled the degree of openness and fronting that they applied to interactions and thus the very dynamics of such relationships.

Although there was little choice as to who one could associate with on a wider level—you had to live with other prisoners on the wing, and you had little control over imbalanced power relationships with staff—individuals could choose how they defined such exchanges, forming closer associations with those with whom they had some degree of affinity, trust, or commonality (and thus whom they were less able or willing to differentiate themselves from). This sometimes resulted in the emergence of informal subcultures within the prison as a result of commonalities such as religion or interest in making music, thus allowing individuals to exert a degree of control over others (and similarly be controlled themselves) through the dynamics of such groupings and their associated values, such as religious gender norms.

On an individual level, positive associations allowed men to control how they were seen by others in a more constructive light—elements of individuality could be shared, emotional toughness could be demonstrated in light of contexts learned, and protection could be given highlighting masculine solidarity and toughness. Negative interactions between prisoners could also be evidence of individuals' control—individuals could influence how they were seen by others either by harmfully imposing control over others, or by differentiating themselves from individuals whom they looked negatively upon—generally those who they felt to lack control over their own lives. As such, some negative associations could undermine an individual's control if he was positioned as the lesser man; however, many spoke of the methods they used to manage those risks and avoid such interactions, and thus control their associative sphere in order to avoid such trouble that could potentially undermine their masculinity and personal effectiveness. One of the key ways through which to control others was through the control of spaces, and thus the manipulation of whom one encountered on a regular basis.

The Control of Spaces

The control of personal space could be seen through the imposition of the self upon prisoners' cells, be that through the use of cleaning as a signifier of differentiation from the prisoner collective, or the use of individualising signifiers and elements of decoration such as photographs, religious elements, or pictures put on the walls. Cleaning one's personal space demonstrated the imposition of control over one's environment, in addition to symbolically removing the 'contaminating' effects of the prison (see Goffman 1961) and the evidence of the lack of individuality of such spaces through their repeated use. Control over space can also be seen through the use of funds within the prison—prisoners can spend their money on signifiers of individuality and identity, be that through cleaning products (see Baer 2005), DVDs, games, or food, all of which can indicate distinctive elements of self and add to the performance of identity and differentiation from the prisoner collective.

Control can also be exerted through a prisoner's choice of cell location within the jail—the wing upon which one is situated can distinctly influence how one is seen by other prisoners and staff. Wings of the prison had distinctive natures, such as the segregation unit, the lifer wing, the induction wing with its shared cells and transient population, or the VDTU[2] wings with their distinctive stance on drugs. Prisoners could manage their risk and thus control their situations to a degree through such locating practices. Protection could be sought on the Vulnerable Prisoners' Wing (or potentially on the segregation wing or in the cell for a short period of time) and thus the risk of bullying or violence directed towards an individual could be controlled. As such, the control of space also links to the control of the body and the self.

---

[2] Voluntary Drug Testing Unit

The Control of the Self

The control of the self can easily be seen in its corporeal manifestations on prisoners' bodies. Evidence of the gym and physical development can be seen through the building of muscles, bodily strength, and fitness. Tattoos show the inscription of the self on the body and, along with self-inflicted scars, are evidence of one of the most fundamental aspects of imposed control over the self through the manipulation of the body's appearance to others and its associated symbolism. Such corporeal management can be used as a means of displaying one's identity and personal control over the self and others—muscles and fitness signify personal strength and toughness, and tattoos are often associated with hardness as well as signifying certain affiliations, be that to the family through the display of loved one's names, or to football clubs and so on. In addition, scars can also symbolise toughness if interpreted as being evidence of one's fighting past.

Personal health can also be inscribed upon the body—signs of illness can have implications for how others view and judge you, as some highlighted with reference to the ill appearance associated with drug-taking behaviours. Cleanliness can also be a signifier to others of the self, signifying the ability of an individual to be independent and take care and control over his own body and image, which can be added to through individualising scents and clothing. In this way, the manipulation of the body allows evidence of relationships of control to be seen, as well as control over which elements of identity an individual values most. The control of the self is also evident in the behaviours expressed by individuals—the setting of aspirations and the attainment of skills and qualifications demonstrate an individual's control over his intended life course, and the ownership of time allows individual prisoners to avoid the feeling of their time being 'wasted' and thus out of their control.

When such avenues of control of others, spaces, and selves were lost or unavailable—particularly when under the restraining influence of the institution—men cited their stresses and frustrations. When other men denounced or were unable to take control over their selves, their sentences, or their spaces, they were defined as weak or vulnerable. What ran throughout these processes of control was the fact that such processes had the aim of appealing to a particular audience that mattered to that individual.

Visibility and the 'Audience That Matters'

In a piece looking at the making of the Mexican nation, Deborah Cohen makes an excellent point that 'in advocating for women's inclusion, we mistakenly assumed that all men were equally visible as citizen-subjects and that exclusion from the nation was based only on gender' (2014: 119). When considered against the backdrop of the prison, the truth of this statement becomes even more apparent. Throughout this book, we have seen how men's access to time, spaces, people, and physical signifiers of legitimate masculinity are generally denied to them (or at least restricted) when in the prison. This in turn relegates incarcerated men to the realm of the feminine: men are not always able to undertake masculine work, but must work in the domestic sphere instead; men are restricted in the spaces that they can go relative to staff members, who grant status to the certain lucky few who can enter spaces of power, and so on. When it comes to spaces in particular, but also arguably applicable to other tropes, femininity in reality means invisibility. The notion of visibility is central to the hegemonic construct of masculinity—there cannot be aspirations to hegemony without someone being clearly visible to align or compare oneself with. We know of men that we ascribe masculine power to because we *see* them. They are visible in their masculinities. Those in society who tend to be invisible—the mentally ill, the poor, the homeless—are conspicuous in their absence both from view and from power and masculine capital.

Men who commit crime may become visible yet invisible: they may have a reputation for their criminality, but are highly invisible to the criminal justice system for the majority of the time (the Kray twins and Al Capone being excellent cases in point). Those men in prison who have been caught are in a remarkable position of becoming visible to some, but being rendered invisible through their positioning within an institution that itself is highly restricted in visibility since the demise in the spectacle of punishment as theorised by Foucault (1975). In this sense, we can see that the internalisation of punishment, and the move away from corporal punishment has had much wider implications for the gendered identities of the men subject to this punishment: when punishment was a spectacle, visibility was high, and therefore so was masculine status of the punished (and the punishers).

Within the prison, however, there is still masculine status, even though the individual becomes invisible to the outside world. The notions of visibility still apply within the prison; the difference is that the audience that matters for the masculine performance has shifted for most of the time from those the individual valued on the outside, such as peers or family, to those who see him on the inside: other prisoners and prison staff. The changes in the audience that matters to the individual are central to the changes in behaviour that accompany imprisonment, and the potential changes in self that prison aspires to impose on men: that is, moving away from crime.

The 'Audience That Matters'

Seeing gender as a social construction and as inherently relational in nature, it becomes clear that, when demonstrating masculinity, men perform their masculinity *for* a particular audience. There are many audiences available to all men to choose from: they may be peers, friends, family, colleagues, superiors, institutions such as the police, and so on; the list is endless. The performances of gender for each audience will be slightly different—we saw this earlier when I reflected upon how men acted with me when alone or when in front of other men. With this in mind, men must *make a choice*. This may not be a conscious choice, but however the process happens, men ascribe different values to different audiences, and this can change across different periods of an individual's life. The 'audience that matters' to that individual changes. It is such audiences that affect men's behaviours, and thus such audiences that can influence behaviour. Young men who offend often do so for reputation amongst their peers (Jamieson et al. 1999; Jackson 2002; Barry 2006, 2007; Weaver 2015), and this can be seen in the different perceptions of YOIs relative to adult prisons: men in adult prisons are much less concerned with the views of their peers. Many would link this to the maturation process and the notion of growing out of crime (Glueck and Glueck 1943, 1950, 1968, 1974; Gottfredson and Hirschi 1990), yet this seems like quite a shift for an individual to do on their own. Indeed, why would you change when such changes require great personal alteration?

If, instead, we think that the people whose opinions matter most to that man change and their feelings about him actually matter to him, then we see that to be a good reason why a young man might move away from crime. Many of the men spoken to in this research spoke about having someone that mattered to them—a partner or a child, for instance—who they wanted to get out of prison for, who they wanted to change for. Yes, the growth in social capital beyond young male peers is aligned with the maturation process, but in many cases, it could be argued that maturation happened *because* of this change in social capital values: because the audience that matters most to the individual changes. This would also explain why those that are married are most likely to desist from crime (Rand 1987; Gibbens 1984; Laub and Sampson 1993; Farington and West 1995; Laub et al. 1998), and why a breakdown in relationships can be quite so devastating for an individual's desistance pathway (Alleyne and Wood 2011; Cid and Martí 2012; Weaver and McNeill 2015).[3] The notion of audiences that matter also goes some way to explaining why only some men commit crimes: it is audience dependent, and some men consciously recognise and try to address this:

Researcher: You also said that you're trying to move away into a different *area*
Logan: Yeah
Researcher: Do you think that's really important?
Logan: Well it's a, it's a fresh start for me [...] Like...a fresh start's always good I believe like...no one's going to know you, no one's going to judge ya, and you can get on with your life, you've got no interferences

---

[3] Many, many thanks to Dr Paula Hamilton for all her help with the desistance literature!

Perhaps a greater focus is needed on encouraging an appreciation for the different audiences that matter to individuals in prison—helping those who do not have people that matter to them, and for whom they might want to move away from crime, to find such links. A good probation officer can always turn into an audience that matters, but with heavy caseloads, risk aversion policies, and privatisation processes as they are, the pressures of the job often make such relationships difficult to achieve. That said, it is crucial to recognise that such relationships with others are one of the only choices that men can make autonomously, and so it needs to be respected as such. The social manipulation of relationships and audiences will merely reimpose feminising and infantilising control processes, and such engineered interactions are unlikely to result in the emotional and behavioural investments indented.

Gender and Visibility

Prison does just about everything possible to render men invisible, and as men are highly visible beings due to the intertwined nature of masculinity and visibility, this results in prisoners often being positioned as 'non-men' relative to those in the outside world (as seen in terms of spatial access, the imposition of cyclical time, and other feminising signifiers noted throughout this book). Thus, men have to make greater efforts to overcome invisibility within the prison, which is why violence and dominance can often occur: these make the individual highly visible and appear hypermasculine, even though they are not necessarily socially acceptable behaviours. Reputation equates to visibility (which is why men can achieve masculine status through crime even if they are not visible in the sense of having been caught, such as Jack the Ripper). The key is that men are visible *to* someone: to a specific audience that matters to him. Domestic violence perpetrators achieve masculinity by performing their dominating and violent behaviours to the audience of their own selves; drug dealers and murderers achieve masculine visibility to the audience that knows them by reputation, and so on.

Being visible to the audience that matters to the individual affects how they behave and how they see themselves as men in terms of hegemonic masculinity. We know that hegemonic masculinity is socially and culturally dependent: it changes with different audiences in time and space, which is why masculinity is such a fluid concept. There is a difference, however, in being visible and being a spectacle: women are spectacles, watched for the benefit of men; men must achieve visibility, but not be feminised in the process (see also Cohan 1993). Sex offenders tend to be seen as spectacles: they have misused their masculinities and become sexual beings (the perceived realm of women), and so are not visible in the masculine sense. In addition, when the audience that matters the most is internalised (as it often is with men who commit sexual offences, with this crime not being granted masculinity by the majority of other men), this can cause problems as men cannot easily grant any masculinity to themselves that other men will automatically recognise. As noted earlier, the outcomes of performances from the audience and the self must align to result in meaningful masculine status. The granting of masculinity that will be seen as currency within groups of other men must come from beyond the individual.

Summary

As has been shown, the male prison (and its associated male-centeredness, monosexuality, and restrictive nature) forces men to seek a variety of ways to assert their gendered identities, which are put under the microscope by others and the masculine self; yet the socially acceptable and legitimate fora for such gendered demonstrations are limited and often dislocated from the outside world that the male prisoner hopes to return to. In this way, prison has a highly manipulative nature when it comes to the encouragement of masculine identity, forcing men to exert control and ownership in performances for the benefit of the self and others, whilst maintaining a balance between how he sees and associates himself, and how distinct groups of others also see him relative to those that he is situated with.

The impact of others in the prison upon the individual and his masculine identity is substantial. Individuals shape and perform their masculine identities for the benefit of the men they live with in order to fit with the gendered expectations of the masculine prisoner collective. Although such expectations are generally internalised within the individual and thus expressions of his own masculine expectations and stereotypes, and thus not regularly policed by the collective, it is the occasional policing of extreme transgressions (often in quite violent or harmful ways) that encourages men to conform to masculine appearances. This was noted in the context of relationships in Chapter 6, whereby individuals will often alter their own behaviours in order to negotiate potentially harmful relationships with others and avoid that could undermine their own masculine credentials, such as fights or situations of bullying.

All this confirms Kimmel's (1994) contention that men are granted their masculinities by other men, making masculinity a form of homophobia through the fact that other men can expose one's lack of masculinity. The fact that such behaviours seem to be exacerbated within the prison, where emotionality is suppressed and the environment and interactions appear to take on hypermasculine appearances, highlights the fact that the single-sexed setting and the associated relationships between men do play a part in shaping male identities and behaviours as seen by others. Many participants spoke of the need to put on a front, and the way that they had to suppress some elements of their identities that could be seen as forms of weakness in front of other male prisoners, yet could act and speak differently when alone in their cells, to their families, or even to me as a female researcher. It is essential not to forget or sideline these other audiences, who also significantly affect the individual's performances, and can have the potential to aid in the desistance process.

Relationships between male prisoners are based upon notions of spectacle—men watch other men in a seemingly unspoken policing of the masculine identity that occurs through the internalisation of the male gaze. Although this gaze does occur on the outside, the fact that the audience within the prison is such a concentration of masculine expectation, and the fact that the tools for legitimate masculine performance are so limited, has the result that men tend to conform to prison stereotypes of emotional toughness and physical hardness, rather than being able to be themselves. As Schmid and Jones (1991) argue, the longer individuals hide their true selves, the less able they may be to readjust to their non-prisoner identities. This may also be due to the fact that long periods in prison can have erosive impacts on relationships with those outside prison (see Hairston 2015).

As has been noted, the impact of imprisonment and the associated immersion within a single-sexed setting has a substantial impact upon the individual and his displayed masculinity—in turn, this has implications for the ways in which individuals interact with others in terms of how they perform their masculine selves in exchanges. The perceived need to retain a tough masculine identity in the eyes of other men has the result of limiting the openness and trust applied to relationships (see Crewe 2009), which in turn alters the characteristics and value applied to such interactions (i.e. being classed as 'associations' instead of 'friendships'). The need to perform in this manner and thus limit the extent of one's non-emphasised or less masculine gendered identity seen by others occurs because of the masculine spotlight (albeit often internalised) men in prison are put under by virtue of their immersion in a single-sexed environment filled with similarly gender-disenfranchised men (i.e. other men who have resorted to criminal behaviour as a means to assert masculine identity—Messerschmidt 1993: 84). In addition, the lack of feminine presence against which individuals can juxtapose their masculinity (Connell 2005: 43–44) results in the need to emphasise individual masculinities that become hierarchised: with a lack of regular femininity against which to situate masculinity, individual masculinities must compete against each other, with some becoming feminised through the application of labels of vulnerability and weakness, whereas others achieve masculine status in relation.

It has become increasingly apparent that prisoners are highly disenfranchised men, lacking in many resources through which to act out their masculine selves legitimately. What seems to be lacking is any formal recognition of the pressures of masculinity upon and from interactions with other prisoners in the ways recognised in the preceding sections. Although there are positive tools for the legitimate performances of masculinity by men with others—such as the relationships of support, relationships of religion, relationships of physicality in the gym and through sports, and the positive informal interactions that occur during association—it would be useful for such encouragement to be expanded within the prison, and more outlets for positive masculine interactions to occur.

Some prisoners spoke of their wish for outlets such as other sports teams or youth-based community projects where they could express their individuality whilst working with others. Individuals also seemed to develop positive relationships with those that they had similar interests with, or with whom they shared developmental prison experiences, going through a joint journey. If this shared development—actually a form of inter-prisoner support, yet distanced from weakness through its shared and developmental nature—could be used more, such as through more group activities and discussions based around signifiers of masculinity (i.e. the work of *Safe Ground*, or the programme discussed by Potts (1996) for West Yorkshire Probation Service), perhaps greater bonds of trust and affinity could be encouraged, thereby reducing the need for performances of masculinity based upon fear of other men.

The book raises the issue of the manner in which men as individuals are affected by their relationships with other men in prison, and vice versa, highlighting the tortuous interplay between the prisoner collective and the prisoner as an individual in gendered terms. On a wider scale, the prison experience as a whole shapes individual prisoners and their behaviours in a number of ways that have been considered in detail: processes of individualism, differentiation, performance, and control in particular. Men experience prison as numerous tests to their masculinity—relationships with others force them to adapt their identities for the benefit of placating others; distancing from the family undermines identities as fathers and partners; time in prison destabilises masculine signifiers in employment, as jobs are lost when incarcerated; and more substantially, independent individuals must now rely on others for the mundane running of their lives.

In an attempt to manage such challenges to their masculine selves, men in prison use 'positive' methods such as differentiation from the prisoner 'other' in order to distance themselves from the negative and stigmatising connotations applied to the identity of "prisoner". Such assertions of individuality both demonstrate men's self-sufficiency and independence in the limited ways available, as well as allow men to emphasise the valuable legitimate signifiers of masculinity in their own lives, such as fatherhood, musical performance, educational advancement, religious status, and so on. Even so, men experience prison as a restrictive setting for the establishment of their masculine selves in such legitimate manners, resulting in the need to assert control over their selves, environments, and others in numerous legitimate and illegitimate ways, all of which go some way towards performing masculinity for the benefit of the particular audience that matters at that point in time.

The prison can be seen to be a microcosm of masculinity—albeit restricted masculinity—demonstrating the implications of disempowerment and a lack of legitimate gender resources for communities of men. Although much of the literature and stereotypes considering prisons centre upon extremes, this research highlights the day-to-day ways that men lacking access to masculine resources and undergoing processes of feminisation attempt to retain their masculine identities in various dimensions of daily life.

Such controlling behaviours can often be seen outside the prison even where men have women against which to situate their gendered selves—in many cases of domestic violence, for example, men take control over women, often due to the disempowerment they feel in aspects of their own lives. This control is a resource through which to distinguish oneself in the masculine world, and is a direct response to gendered disempowerment when masculine opportunities are apparently restricted to an individual. A greater understanding of this and the pressures men experience on their identities can help in the understanding of such harmful manifestations of masculinity, as well as in suggesting the reasons behind illegitimate male behaviours. Examining men in the prison setting puts masculine disempowerment under the microscope—in prison, masculinities are exacerbated and pushed to extremes due to the mental and emotional pressures a prisoner experiences in combination with a lack of masculine tools, an intense masculine gaze, and the need to show manhood without women.

Final Thoughts

In this book, I have focused upon the subject of masculinities in prison, and have tried to look at men in terms of who they are as men—beyond merely their prison selves. I have privileged the variable of masculinity above other differentiating elements such as age, race, ethnicity, and so on, as masculinity and maleness is the variable shared by all the partici-pants—and 95% of the prison population in England and Wales. Being male is the most pervasive character of the entire prison population. Despite the dominance of masculinity in prisons, a host of other variables have tended to be highlighted in the existing academic work regarding prisoners. This other work is vital in understanding the prison system and prisoners' experiences and interpretations of it, and was highly influential on the focus and design of this research (see, for example, Jewkes 2002a, b; Crewe 2005a, b, 2006a, b, 2007, 2009, 2011; Phillips 2012; Phillips and Earle 2010). Although this existing work is all highly influential, the missing link generally failing throughout to reach centre-stage in lieu of a host of other important variables is that these research subjects are men. As such, and as this book suggests, the use of gender might allow the cross-fertilisation of such research and connect the wide variety of academic thoughts on the area of incarceration. Although all of these fabulous examples did mention gender within their work, this was rarely the central focus, as it is in this book.

What I attempt to bring to the academic table is just that often under-privileged (or sometimes totally missing) connecting link, which is essen-tial to producing a holistic body of knowledge. Moreover, I not only consider the maleness of prisoners and how their gender is negotiated when in isolation from other gendered norms and influences, but I also explore the effects that this can have on and within the prison as an insti-tution. In addition, I gender the research process itself with a focus upon the implications for both the researcher and research participants of a woman interviewing men.

My approach has highlighted what connects men in prison (such as tropes of control, visibility, and the value of certain audiences in the mas-culine process), rather than what distinguishes them from each other, in the hope that through understanding the whole as a dynamic collection, the impacts of imprisonment upon masculinity—and vice versa—can be better understood. In fact, through understanding masculinity in such a distinctive setting, it is possible to consider in more detail the condition of masculinity as a whole, and perhaps to understand men generally and the pressures they experience better. By understanding more about mas-culinity in isolation, fragile gendered power relations and differentials are exposed. Removing (to a degree at least) men from the diverse range of heterosexual power relations that are available in the outside world, we can see how many of the ways in which men deal with the performative limitations of such a restricted gender environment do not conform to the hypermasculine model of masculinity that many perceive prison to apply. Men in prison often invest their time and emotions in the intimate, the domestic, the emotive, the body-centric, and the vulnerable—areas that are traditionally seen to be the reserve of femininity. This shows us much more about the flexible and contextual nature of gendered identity as a whole, and the interplay between gender and agency in people's lives.

Through undertaking this research, I have learned a number of things, beyond the actual findings of the research elaborated upon in the preceding chapters, and further than the importance of considering gender in one's methodological approach. What I have discovered, is that *men are men* regardless of their location or personal circumstances or other identity variables. Some events and environments compel certain gendered responses by virtue of internalised and/or externalised gender-based behavioural policing or responses. Hegemonic masculinities result in internalised expectations placed upon the gendered self as seen through the lens of the audience that matters, and these internalised cultural and values of masculinity change according to the audience of value to that particular man at that particular time. In addition, through the process of interviewing men about their lives, experiences, and perceptions of imprisonment; through immersing myself within the prison setting and watching what goes on within; and through talking to people about the research and reflecting upon my own experiences in an effort to be reflective and reflexive, I have learned one central and overarching thing. Prison places extremely high expectations upon people, and can subsequently cause serious damage (Behan 2002)—particularly to their (gendered) identities and selves.

The masculine expectations imposed upon prisoners by other prisoners (and arguably staff) can have implications in terms of the collective shaping the individual in ways that are inconsistent with the expectations of society outside prison. The masculine norms expected of male prisoners are often manifested in socially illegitimate ways. This is in part, as Messerschmidt (1993) notes, a result of such men's lack of access to legitimate means through which to 'do' their masculinities, thus having to resort to criminality. However, I would argue that this research shows that such manifestations are also the result of gendered behaviours that are collectively expected (and thereby enforced) within the prison environment (and arguably, before). Although these can be due to the deprivations of prison (Sykes 1958), they are also the result of the sheer number of men confined together under an almost wholly masculine gaze. Such a gaze requires masculinity to be demonstrated for the achievement of manliness, which is granted by men to men (Kimmel 1994), and this can be done through a number of illegitimate and legitimate means, all of which are available to all prisoners in some form or another.

Such performances also sit in tension with performances undertaken for the benefit of other audiences who matter to the individual (including the self). With this in mind, Messerschmidt's (1993) suggestion that crime is a result of a lack of other means through which to perform masculinity legitimately requires some amendment. In the prison setting, it is more likely that illegitimate means are often *easier* ways through which to acquire a masculine reputation, yet the main way to demonstrate manliness is through the imposition of *control.* Such control may be over others and the relationships one has with them, one's environment—be that geographical, emotional, or temporal—or one's self through processes of performance or differentiation. The performance of one's masculinity through the imposition of control has both positive and negative implications, but, as has been noted, the easiest means are often through illegitimate or harmful behaviours, which in turn have potentially negative implications for release and reintegration.

In other words, if men in the free world have to resort to crime as a means through which to perform their masculinities as a result of other legitimate means being unavailable to them (Messerschmidt 1993), and then when in prison are encouraged to demonstrate their manliness through the imposition of control in some form or another—a mechanism that has restricted masculine appeal in the free world and thus limited transferability upon release—then male prisoners are at a key disadvantage. As this book has discussed, some individuals are unable to (or opt not to) conform to the masculine norms imposed through the male gaze of other prisoners, be that through their inability to show control over themselves, their spaces, or others, or through their failure to differentiate themselves from the prisoner collective. When individuals fail to perform masculinity within the relatively restrictive limits available to them (or expected of them) they enter the realm of vulnerability—either through their being located in this category through the eyes of others (an excellent demonstration of labelling theory in action [see Becker 1966: 179]), or through personal association with vulnerability through internalised weaknesses.

Some men who could be seen to be vulnerable avoid the label through their association with forms of strength and control by virtue of their criminal pasts, their prisoner selves, or their coping capabilities and ability to compensate for and cover up potential weaknesses. For those individuals who avoid being attributed with labels of vulnerability, the men that they are valorised as being inside prison can rarely be similarly appreciated outside—in fact, the 'prison men' are often—by virtue of their prisoner identities—prevented from such legitimate valour or the means through which to become legitimate 'free men'. The audience who matters has changed and the masculine capital situated within one audience is rarely easily transferable to another.

The overarching message that I hope is taken from this book is as follows: the nuances of men's subjective masculinities and lives need to be considered more when punishing in order to punish meaningfully and suitably—otherwise we just damage them. The criminal justice system does not need to restrict and erode masculinity to the degree that it does: that merely equates to fighting fire with fire. Instead, masculinities can be directed in line with people that these men value and want to improve their lives for, and previously negative masculine behaviours can be redirected towards meaningful, useful jobs, more education, more family ties, and so on. In reality, prisons should be less about security: essentially masculinity battling masculinity (and assuming masculinity to be violent in the process, as also recognised by Phillips 2012). Instead, we need to renegotiate the whole notion of 'boys will be boys' and the expectations that we place on men—young and old. Otherwise, we merely set up men to fail, and push them towards finding value and visibility from less socially acceptable—more criminal—sources. Perhaps we need to do more as a society to encourage positive relationships and development of meaningful audiences that matter to men, and enable those who struggle to be visible as men to do so in more socially acceptable ways. Otherwise, how else can we expect criminal men to really make a change and—perhaps most importantly—to want to?

References

Alleyne, E., & Wood, J. L. (2011). Gang membership: The psychological evidence. In F.-A. Esbensen & C. L. Maxson (Eds.), *Youth gangs in international perspective: Findings from the Eurogang Program of Research*. New York: Springer.

Baer, L. D. (2005). Visual imprints on the prison landscape: A study on the decorations in prison cells. *Tijdschrift voor Economische en Sociale Geografie, 96*(2), 209–217.

Barry, M. (2006). *Youth offending in transition: The search for social recognition*. Abingdon: Routledge.

Barry, M. (2007). Youth offending and youth transitions: The power of capital in influencing change. *Critical Criminology, 15*(2), 185–199.

Becker, H. S. (1966). *Outsiders: Studies in the sociology of deviance* (Newth ed.). New York: The Free Press.

Behan, C. (2002). *Transformative learning in a total institution*. Unpublished MA Dissertation, National University of Ireland, Maynooth.

Cid, J., & Martí, J. (2012). Turning points and returning points: Understanding the role of family ties in the process of desistance. *European Journal of Criminology, 9*(6), 603–620.

Cohan, S. (1993). 'Feminising' the song-and-dance man: Fred Astaire and the spectacle of masculinity in the Hollywood musical. In S. Cohan & I. R. Hark (Eds.), *Screening the male: Exploring masculinities in Hollywood cinema*. London and New York: Routlegde.

Cohen, D. (2014). Masculinity and social visibility: Migration, state spectacle, and the making of the Mexican nation. *Estudios Interdisciplinarios de América Latina y el Caribe, 16*(1), 119–132.

Connell, R. W. (2005). *Masculinities* (2nd ed.). Cambridge: Polity Press.

Connell, R. W., & Messerschmidt, J. W. (2005). Hegemonic masculinity: Rethinking the concept. *Gender and Society, 19*(6), 829–859.

Crewe, B. (2005a). Prisoner society in the era of hard drugs. *Punishment and Society, 7*(4), 457–481.

Crewe, B. (2005b). Codes and conventions: The terms and conditions of contemporary inmate values. In A. Liebling & S. Maruna (Eds.), *The effects of imprisonment*. Cullompton: Willan Publishing.

Crewe, B. (2006a). The drugs economy and the prisoner society. In Y. Jewkes & H. Johnston (Eds.), *Prison readings: A critical introduction to prisons and imprisonment*. Cullompton: Willan Publishing.

Crewe, B. (2006b). Prison drug dealing and the ethnographic lens. *The Howard Journal, 45*(4), 347–368.

Crewe, B. (2007). Power, adaptation and resistance in a late modern men's prison. *British Journal of Criminology, 47*(2), 256–275.

Crewe, B. (2009). *The prisoner society: Power, adaptation, and social life in an English prison.* Oxford, New York: Oxford University Press.

Crewe, B. (2011). Depth, weight, tightness: Revisiting the pains of imprisonment. *Punishment and Society, 13*(5), 509–529.

Farrington, D.P. and West, D.J., 1995. Effects of marriage, separation, and children on offending by adult males. *Current perspectives on aging and the life cycle, 4*, pp.249-281.

Foucault, M. (1975). *Discipline and punish: The birth of the prison.* London, New York, Victoria, Ontario and Auckland: Penguin Books.

Gibbens, T. C. (1984). Borstal boys after 25 years. *British Journal of Criminology, 24*, 46–59.

Glueck, S., & Glueck, E. (1943). *Criminal careers in retrospect.* New York: Commonwealth Fund.

Glueck, S., & Glueck, E. (1950). *Unravelling juvenile delinquency.* New York: Commonwealth Fund.

Glueck, S., & Glueck, E. (1968). *Delinquents and nondelinquents in perspective.* Cambridge, MA: Harvard University Press.

Glueck, S., & Glueck, E. (1974). *Of delinquency and crime.* Springfield, IL: Charles C. Thomas.

Goffman, E. (1961). *Asylums: Essays on the social situation of mental patients and other inmates.* Chicago: Aldine Publishing Company.

Gottfredson, M., & Hirschi, T. (1990). *A general theory of crime.* Stanford, CA: Stanford University Press.

Hairston, C. F. (2015). Family ties during imprisonment: Important to whom and for what? *The Journal of Sociology & Social Welfare, 18*(1), 6, 87–104.

Irwin, J. (1970). *The felon.* New Jersey: Prentice-Hall, Inc.

Jackson, C. (2002). 'Laddishness' as a self-worth protection strategy. *Gender and Education, 14*(1), 37–50.

Jamieson, J., McIvor, G, & Murray, C. (1999). *Understanding offending among young people- research findings.* Scottish Executive. Social Work Findings 37, Scottish Executive Central Research Unit.

Jewkes, Y. (2002a). The use of media in constructing identities in the masculine environment of men's prisons. *European Journal of Communication, 17*(2), 205–225.

Jewkes, Y. (2002b). *Captive audience: Media, masculinity and power in prisons.* Cullompton: Willan Publishing.

Kaufman, M. (1994). Men, feminism, and men's contradictory experiences of power. In H. Brod & M. Kaufman (Eds.), *Theorizing masculinities*. Thousand Oaks, London and New Delhi: Sage Publications, Inc.

Kimmel, M. S. (1994). Masculinity as homophobia: Fear, shame, and silence in the construction of gender identity. In H. Brod & M. Kaufman (Eds.), *Theorizing masculinities*. Thousand Oaks and London: Sage.

Koss, M. P., Goodman, L., Fitzgerald, L., Russo, N. F., Keita, G. P., & Browne, A. (1994). *No safe haven: Male violence against women at home, at work and in the community*. Washington, DC: American Psychological Association.

Laub, J. H., Nagin, D. S., & Sampson, R. J. (1998). Trajectories of change in criminal offending: Good marriages and the desistance process. *American Sociological Review, 63*, 225–238.

Laub, J. H., & Sampson, R. J. (1993). Turning points in the life course: Why change matters in the study of crime. *Criminology, 31*, 301–325.

Messerschmidt, J. W. (1993). *Masculinities and crime*. Maryland: Rowman and Littlefield Publishers, Inc.

Odih, P. (1999). Gendered time in the age of deconstruction. *Time and Society, 8*(1), 9–38.

Phillips, C. (2012). *The multicultural prison: Ethnicity, masculinity and social relations among prisoners*. Oxford: Oxford University Press.

Phillips, C., & Earle, R. (2010). Reading difference differently? Identity, epistemology and prison ethnography. *British Journal of Criminology, 50*(2), 360–378.

Rand, A. (1987). Transitional life events and desistance from delinquency and crime. In M. Wolfgang, T. P. Thornberry, & R. M. Figlio (Eds.), *From boy to man: From delinquency to crime*. Chicago: Chicago University Press.

Schmid, T. J., & Jones, R. S. (1991). Suspended Identity: Identity transformation in a maximum security prison. *Symbolic Interaction, 14*(4), 415–432.

Sykes, G. (1958). *The society of captives: A study of a maximum security prison* (2007th ed.). Princeton, NJ: Princeton University Press.

The Chambers Dictionary. (2003). *Ninth edition*. Edinburgh: Chambers Harrap Publishers Ltd.

Weaver, B. (2015). *Offending and desistance: The importance of social relations*. Abingdon: Routledge.

Weaver, B., & McNeill, F. (2015). Lifelines: Desistance, social relations and reciprocity. *Criminal Justice and Behaviour, 42*(1), 95–107.

Afterword

To place men under the spotlight, and to problematize masculinity, is not to say that men are of greater concern than other groups or variables within the prison system, nor that all masculinities in prison are inherently negative, nor that all men are problems. Neither does this book intend to say that women must pander to the needs of men, or that men's crime desistance is in any way women's fault or under their control: it is not. Individuals are responsible for their own offending behaviours. Men cannot dominate the criminal justice system and shift the blame for such domination onto others. What the book does try to do, however, is to bring to the fore the aspects of male incarceration that dominates all systems all over the world, and attempt to unpack how prisons and masculinities interact and intertwine. What I wish to bring attention to is the fact that men make their own choices as to how they behave, and such choices are as a result of the people around them, and the amount of value that they place upon that audience's opinions and views of them as an individual—even if those opinions are only the internalised perceptions of that individual man himself. Ultimately, this book tries to make visible both the wood and the trees in the prison landscape.

© The Editor(s) (if applicable) and The Author(s) 2016   **183**
J.A. Sloan, *Masculinities and the Adult Male Prison Experience*,
DOI 10.1057/978-1-137-39915-1

Bibliography

Banbury, S. (2004). Coercive sexual behaviour in British prisons as reported by adult ex-prisoners. *The Howard Journal of Criminal Justice, 43*(2), 113–130.

Bennett, T. (1998). *Drugs and crime: The results of research on drug testing and interviewing arrestees* (Home Office Research Study 183). London: Home Office.

Drake, D. H., Earle, R., & Sloan, J. (Eds.). (2015). *The Palgrave handbook of prison ethnography*. Basingstoke: Palgrave Macmillan.

Fitzclarence, L., & Hickey, C. (2001). Real footballers don't eat quiche: Old narratives in new times. *Men and Masculinities, 4*(2), 118–139.

Gear, S. (2001, April 4–7). *Sex, sexual violence and coercion in men's prisons*. Paper presented at AIDS in Context International Conference. Retrieved November, 2015 from http://www.heart-intl.net/HEART/070106/Sex, SexualViolence.htm

Gear, S. (2005). Behind the bars of South African prisons: Gendered roles and vulnerability of male inmates to forced sex. *Sexual Health Exchange*, 2005–2. Retrieved July, 2011 from http://www.kit.nl/exchange/html/2005-2_behind_the_bars_of_sout.asp

Gear, S. (2007). Behind the bars of masculinity: Male rape and homophobia in and about South African men's prisons. *Sexualities, 10*(2), 209–227.

Geltner, G. (2008). Coping in medieval prisons. *Continuity and Change, 23*(1), 151–172.

© The Editor(s) (if applicable) and The Author(s) 2016
J.A. Sloan, *Masculinities and the Adult Male Prison Experience*,
DOI 10.1057/978-1-137-39915-1

Heidensohn, F., Silvestri, M., & Campling, J. (1985). *Women and crime.* London: Macmillan.

HM Inspectorate of Prisons. (2007). *Time out of cell: A short thematic review.* London: HM Inspectorate of Prisons.

HM Prison Service Statement of Purpose. Retrieved November, 2015 from http://webarchive.nationalarchives.gov.uk/20110505130548/http://www.hmprisonservice.gov.uk/abouttheservice/statementofpurpose/

Hulley, S., Crewe, B., & Wright, S. (2015). Re-examining the problems of long-term imprisonment. *British Journal of Criminology,* In press.

Jack, R. (1992). *Women and attempted suicide.* Hove: Lawrence Erlbaum Associates.

Kennedy, E. (2000). "You Talk a Good Game": Football and masculine style on British television. *Men and Masculinities, 3*(1), 57–84.

Liebling, A. (1995). Vulnerability and prison suicide. *British Journal of Criminology, 35*(2), 173–187.

Lilleaas, U.-B. (2007). Masculinities, sport, and emotions. *Men and Masculinities, 10*(1), 39–53.

Martin, W. B. (1927). The development of psychoses in prison. *Journal of the American Institute of Criminal Law and Criminology, 18*(3), 404–415.

Ministry of Justice. (2009). *Story of the prison population 1995-2009 England and Wales* (Ministry of justice statistics bulletin). London: Ministry of Justice.

Phillips, C. (2007). Ethnicity, identity and community cohesion in prison. In M. Wetherall, M. Lafleche, & R. Berkeley (Eds.), *Identity, ethnic diversity and community cohesion.* London, Thousand Oaks, New Delhi and Singapore: Sage Publications Ltd.

Robinson, V. (2008). *Everyday masculinities and extreme sport: Male identity and rock climbing.* Oxford and New York: Berg.

Sloan, J. (2011). *Men inside: Masculinity and the adult male prison experience.* Unpublished PhD Thesis, University of Sheffield.

Stevens, A. (2015). *Sex in prison: experiences of former prisoners. London: Howard League for Penal Reform, Commission on Sex in Prison.* London, GB, Commission on Sex in Prison.

Struckman-Johnson, C., & Struckman-Johnson, D. (2000). Sexual coercion rates in seven Midwestern prison facilities for men. *The Prison Journal, 80*(4), 379–390.

Wheaton, B. (2000). "New Lads"?: Masculinities and the "New Sport" participant. *Men and Masculinities, 2*(4), 434–456.

Index

© The Editor(s) (if applicable) and The Author(s) 2016
J.A. Sloan, *Masculinities and the Adult Male Prison Experience*,
DOI 10.1057/978-1-137-39915-1